Medical, Legal, & Workplace Issues

for the Transsexual

A Guide for
Successful Transformation

Male to Female
Female to Male

Sheila Kirk, M.D.
Martine Rothblatt, J.D.

Together Lifeworks®

D1509202

Medical, Legal and Workplace Issues For The Transsexual
A Guide For Transformation

Copyright ©1995 Together Lifeworks

ISBN 1-887796-00-2

Published by:

Together Lifeworks ®
P.O. Box 38114
Blawnox, PA 15238

ABOUT THE AUTHORS:

Sheila Kirk, M.D.

As a board certified obstetrician - gynecologist with over 25 years of medical experience in both private practice and research and as a transgendered person herself, Dr. Sheila Kirk is in a unique position to help the transgendered community improve their overall physical and emotional well-being while providing insight and instruction to the medical professionals who administer their care.

During her years specializing in ob/gyn care in a major U.S. city, Dr. Kirk delivered over 8,000 babies; performed hundreds of surgeries ranging from reconstructive gynecological concerns to infertility problems and became a leading expert in hormonal therapy for the pre-menopausal and post-menopausal biologic woman and the transgendered population.

In 1996, Dr. Kirk began specializing in transgender medical and surgical care in Pittsburgh, PA. She performs GRS and related surgeries (i.e. hysterectomies, top surgeries, orchiectomies, breast augmentations) for MTF and FTM individuals as well as administers non-op, pre-op and post-op transgender care and hormonal therapy in her gender clinic.

In 1997, Dr. Kirk became the first transgendered physician to be elected to the board of directors of the Harry Benjamin International Gender Dysphoria Association. She co-established a committee of Advocacy and Liaison to encourage better communication between the T community and professionals. "For the first time, we have a unified opportunity to be heard by the professionals who administer our care and set the standards upon which our care is given," said Dr. Kirk, "As a transgendered physician who in my private practice specializes in caring for our community, I am gratified for this opportunity to work together to make a positive impact through this first and important step in improving our community's welfare."

For over twenty years, Dr. Kirk served as Assistant Clinical Professor, lecturer and consultant at a major university medical school, teaching and supervising medical students and residents in obstetrics and gynecology. On several occasions throughout those years, she was recognized as Teacher of the Year by both the medical students and resident staff. She considers these awards amongst the highest honors she has received. In 1998, she accepted a clinical professorship in the University of Minnesota's Program for Human Sexuality in association with the Department of Family Practice and Community Health. She has also co-edited a book with University of Minnesota's Dr. Walter Bockting that deals with HIV risk, prevention and management in the Transgender Community.

One of Dr. Kirk's primary interests is in generating and promoting research in a number of areas regarding the care of the transgendered person. Currently, Dr. Kirk is conducting two on-going research projects dealing with the teen-age transgendered person and the post-operative M-F Transsexual. In addition, she is currently in the process of developing research in contragender hormonal therapy as it relates to lipid profiles and breast and prostate problems in the transgendered individual.

A noted author and lecturer, Dr. Kirk has written numerous books, articles and research findings on transgendered care as well as other medical concerns in her chosen discipline.

Sought after worldwide as a leading authority on transgendered issues, Dr. Kirk, lectures extensively at universities, medical conferences and symposiums both nationally and internationally.

In addition to her board membership with the Harry Benjamin International Association for Gender Dysphoria, Dr. Kirk serves on the editorial staff of AEGIS, and is a columnist for several T sources including *Transgender Forum, FTM International,* and *Femme Mirror.*

Feel free to contact Dr. Kirk by phone: (412) 781-1092, fax: (412) 781-1096, e-mail: SheilaKirk@aol.com or snail mail: P.O. Box 38114, Blawnox, PA. 15238.

Other Publications by Sheila Kirk, M.D.:

Feminizing Hormonal Therapy for the Transgendered
  ©1996 Sheila Kirk, M.D., Blawnox, PA
  ISBN 1-887796-01-0
  Together Lifeworks®, Blawnox, PA

Masculinizing Hormonal Therapy for the Transgendered
  ©1996 Sheila Kirk, M.D., Blawnox, PA
  ISBN 1-887796-01-0
  Together Lifeworks®, Blawnox, PA

Physician's Guide To Transgendered Medicine, Sheila Kirk, M.D
  ©1996 Together Lifeworks®, Blawnox, PA
  ISBN 1-887796-03-7
  Together Lifeworks®, Blawnox, PA

Hormones - Male to Female
 ©1994 edition Sheila Kirk, M.D.
 (English/German/French/Spanish Translations)
 Together Lifeworks®
 Blawnox, PA

Hormones - Female to Male
 ©1994 edition Sheila Kirk, M.D.
 (English/German/French/Spanish Translations)
 Together Lifeworks®
 Blawnox, PA

Hormonal Treatment For The Transsexual-An Overview For The Professional (audio cassette)
 ©1994 Sheila Kirk, M.D.
 Together Lifeworks®
 Blawnox, PA

Hormones-Male To Female, Female To Male
 ©1991,1992 editions Sheila Kirk, M.D.
 International Foundation For Gender Education,
 Waltham, MA

How To Find A Physician
 ©1989 Sheila Kirk, M.D.
 International Foundation For Gender Education,
 Waltham, MA

How To Be A Good Medical Consumer
 ©1989 Sheila Kirk, M.D.
 International Foundation For Gender Education,
 Waltham, MA

Martine Aliana Rothblatt, J.D.

Martine Aliana Rothblatt, J.D., M.B.A. is an expert on business and regulatory aspects of satellite communications, a leading writer in the field of gender law and social policy, and the Vice-Chair of the International Bar Association's Bio-ethics Sub-committee.

Ms. Rothblatt pioneered the use of satellites for international broadcasting and for mobile communications. In 1984 she successfully petitioned the Federal Communications Commission for its first approval ever for a private international satellite television system, PanAmSat, based on her graduate thesis work of that name at UCLA. As head of Geostar Corp. from 1985-1989, Ms. Rothblatt led the company into launching three satellite systems and equipping thousands of trucks with Sony and Hughes mobile data terminals.

In 1990, she formed Marcor Inc., which over the next few years crated two new mobile communications products: compact disk quality radio broadcasting via satellite (CD Radio) and satellite tracking of public transit vehicles. During 1991-92 Marcor led the first project to use satellites as part of an intelligent vehicle-highway system (Dallas Area Rapid Transit). Since 1993 she has worked to implement the WorldSpace global satellite radio broadcasting system.

Ms. Rothblatt has been instrumental in creating two new international laws which expand satellite communications. the first treaty, approved in 1987, created the radio frequency allocation which Motorola is using for global cellular telephony via satellite. The second treaty, signed in 1992, authorized the use of satellites for broadcasting international radio programming directly to listeners.

Ms. Rothblatt has published over 30 articles and one book on business, legal and technical aspects of state-of-the-art satellite communications systems. She has been elected into life membership of the International Institute of Space Law and the International Academy of Astronautics. She has also taught telecom policy at UCLA, University of Maryland and George Washington University.

In 1981, Ms. Rothblatt earned her Juris Doctor (Order of the Coif) and MBA degrees from UCLA, and her BA (Summa cum Laude) in Communications from UCLA in 1977. After graduating she represented the television broadcasting industry, the National Academy of Sciences and NASA in radio frequency matters before the US Federal Communications Commission, and then entered the satellite industry in 1983.

Ms. Rothblatt is of Counsel to the Washington, D.C. law firm of Mahon & Patusky, Vice-Chair of the International Bar Association's Bioethics Subcommittee, and author of the highly acclaimed book The Apartheid of Sex: A Manifesto on the Freedom of Gender.

She, her spouse and four children live near Washington, D.C.

Other Publications by Martine Aliana Rothblatt, J.D.:

BOOKS

The Apartheid of Sex: A Manifesto on the Freedom of Gender
Crown, 1995.

Radio Satellite Services & Standards
Artech, 1987.

ARTICLES & PAPERS

Transsexual and Transgender Health Law,
16 *Journal of Gender Studies* 24, 1994.

Advising Clients with Transgender Legal Issues in the 1990s,
18 *International Legal Practitioner* 113, 1993.

An American Perspective on Transgender Health Law,
Proceedings of the XXIIIrd Colloquy on European Law: Transsexualism, Medicine and the Law,
Council of Europe, Amsterdam, 1993.

Transgender Health Law,
Proceedings of the First International Conference on Transgender Law and Employment Policy, Houston, 1992.

This book is dedicated to the spouses

of both authors - Pamela and Bina.

What we accomplish, what we have become,

what we will achieve in the future,

is because of their support and their love.

Table of Contents

Preface

PART I   MEDICAL ISSUES

PART II LEGAL ISSUES

PART III WORKPLACE ISSUES

Acknowledgments

I would like to acknowledge an intellectual debt to several people who helped me understand the nature of transgenderism. First, I am grateful to Sandy Stone for her classic essay The Empire Strikes Back: A Post-Transsexual Manifesto. She observed that after spending much of our lives with our future in a closet, it is foolish to spend our post-transition lives with our past in a closet. Second, I am thankful to Leslie Feinberg for his revolutionary monograph, Transgender Liberation. This booklet is the first true history of our people, and is the best single basis I have seen for our collective pride. Leslie helped me feel proud to be transgendered. Third, I am indebted to Dr. Renee Richards for her incredible courage in fighting back in the 1970s and in the often cruel glare of world media attention, for the right to self-define one's sexual identity via hormones and surgery. Her lawsuit, Richards v United States Tennis Association, established the key legal precedent that birth sex can be changed. Her book, Second Serve, broke many unfair, extraordinarily limiting stereotypes of transsexuals. It shows that transsexuals were also star athletes and respected opthamologists. Fourth, I feel a sense of tremendous kinship with Kate Bornstein. Kate tirelessly and brilliantly demonstrates in her book Gender Outlaw and her several plays that "male or female" is a false choice. It's a message that resonates throughout my soul. Last, and never least, I am ever so appreciated of the transgender activism efforts of Phyllis Randolph Frye, Esq. Her example of coming out as openly transgendered in Houston, Texas during the 1970s (when it was actually illegal!) helped unleash my own gender freedom in the 1990s. Her several volume Proceedings of the International Conference on Transgender Law and Employment Policy is must-reading for any transgendered person. To agitate for gender freedom in the halls of Congress or the corridors of your Statehouse, fax Ms. Frye at 713-723-1800.

I am also thankful for the internet generally, and America On Line in particular. The net is a vital communications link among transgendered people worldwide. Type in "transgender" on a web browser and you will enter into a vast realm of information. America On Line has been particularly instrumental in its outreach to the gay, lesbian, bisexual and transgender communities. The transgender bulletin boards on America On Line have literally thousands of postings reflecting the transitioning experiences of countless people. My web address is http://www.webworqs.com/gender3.html. My internet address is gender3@aol.com. See ya in cyberspace, and have a gender friendly day!

Best of Luck,
Martine

I extend deep gratitude to the many individuals who have done so much to assist and prepare in the writing of this book. Many thanks go to Lori who worked on earlier manuscripts taking my illegible words and indistinct dictation and making it all clear and acceptable.

My readers, Karin and Pamela were heaven-sent. Their contribution in correcting language and restating concepts and thought was invaluable. In particular, Pamela spent countless hours in assisting me to mold and reform the huge amount of material that appears here. Her patience and very intelligent advice is most appreciated. And her love and total acceptance of me as her Life Partner and Best Friend has filled me with such joy and completeness.

To Stacey I extend deep, heartfelt gratitude for her skill and experience in the formatting of this book.

Ultimately it is the transgendered community to whom I owe the most. The countless individuals who have shared with me their desires, their disappointments, their joys and accomplishments. They have inspired me to research for them, to assemble information for them and to serve them in placing this information and advice before our community and the medical profession that serves them.

Thank you to all my transgendered Sisters and Brothers.

With warm appreciation,
Sheila

Preface

This book was conceived with the earnest desire to give to the transsexual individual guidelines and assistance as he or she moves through this very special time in their lives. We have taken three distinct periods in which we feel special problems should be addressed and discussed. These are:

1. The transition period or time of real life test.
2. The surgical experience and the immediate hospital convalescence.
3. The late convalescence and life thereafter.

Medical, legal and work place concerns and problems that occur in these periods of time are identified and discussed as they appear in these time frames. Quite a lot has been written for the transsexual about some of these considerations, but often with fiction or myth associated and always inconclusive and limited.

Our intent is to reach out to you with accuracy and with a scope that will leave very little untouched and unconsidered. There is a lot to be covered, and while there is a great deal you may know, we hope to consolidate your knowledge and your thinking in order to help you formulate good planning for these very special times in your life.

We want to emphasize one thing -- what we relate to you tends to be our formulas for the best results. Keep in mind however, your professional in medicine and law and your employer may have a different approach. They may at times feel that they have a method or plan that works very well in their hands and is best for you and that is certainly possible. Hence, we don't want to impose a rigidity upon you or a sense that there is only one way for you to reach your goals and accomplish your plans. To give you some things to consider and offer in discussion with your professional or employer and to add to your education is our purpose.

You should be prepared with special knowledge of what to expect while in the evaluation period and what inquiries will be made of you. What you and your therapist and others in your team will look for, ask for, and want to know is what we will discuss with you in these chapters to follow. At the same time, we will coordinate your medical experience with what you will need to know about legal and civil matters.

In addition, it is most important that you know what you are apt to experience in the work place. To give you the background needed to relate productively, comfortably and efficiently with your employer and companion employees, to be able to do your work and to do it productively, is another very important area of discussion.

When the surgical time period is discussed, for example, we want to give you insight into your personal preparation for surgery, some idea of what the surgery is all about and to explain what you will experience once surgery is completed. When you are in convalescence it is important for you to know some of what could take place. Certainly some of this may be modified by your own surgeon, for not every surgeon does reassignment in the same way and their after surgical care may be somewhat different from what you have been told by friends who have been through that process.

Principles are the same however and certain experiences in convalescence can be in common. You should know what possibilities there are. There may be important legal and work place considerations for you to have looked into or prepared for during this time.

Once out of the hospital and healing at home, while preparing for your life thereafter, there are certain medical hurdles you may encounter, and here, once again, will be the need to consider certain legal and work place issues. All in all, this book should serve as a companion -- a map to guide you to becoming a new and successful person. It should serve to aid you in continuing your life with contentment and with as little complication as possible.

There are areas in the material to follow which pertain only to the Male to Female and some only to the Female to Male individual. There are some that are written and directed to both at the same time. The letters M-F/F-M will be found next to a heading that deals with topics common to both. Special sections for just the Male to Female or Female to Male will be so indicated by the heading and by a letter designation. For Male to Female, M-F will be the designation, for Female to Male, F-M will be indicated.

We hope what we relate to you is very helpful and we sincerely wish you success in what you seek to accomplish.

Please understand that some sections may seem to be repetitive. This may be tiresome if you read both the F-M and M-F sections. In order to give important information to those who read only in the sections pertaining to them and not the whole book, those repetitions are necessary.

Sheila Kirk, M.D.
Martine Aliana Rothblatt, J.D.

PART 1

Medical Issues

SHEILA KIRK, M.D.

*"Anatomic sex and even chromosomal sex
are not the last or most important designations. . .
Gender identity is"*

A- The Pre-transition Period -M-F/F-M

During this time evaluation by the mental health-care professional is necessary and important. Many demands will be made of the client to assure, to prove, to establish the fact that hormonal therapy and eventual surgery is the correct step. The knowledge that this is an irreversible action is a warranted and necessary concept to be emphasized. If other psychologic pathology is uncovered in the process then solutions and alternatives to these difficulties will be worked through to make certain the gender identity question is being managed in the right way and with remarkable clarity. The client must understand this.

There are mutual responsibilities that both client and evaluator should recognize. The client must be cooperative and adhere to the criteria laid out before him or her. Of course there will be room to object, discuss and negotiate, but in the main the system should be followed as outlined by the evaluator. The mental health-care professional on the other hand, while posing as an obstructionist in order to search out and clarify, should in time add therapy and support as well as direction to the interchange between the two. I know of counselors who continue to place one impediment after another even when the tests and examinations clearly indicate the client is on the correct path. I know of transsexuals who refuse to accept what is told to them or what is asked of them. It is not at all a battle. There must be a cooperative effort, offered by both.

The pre-transition evaluation time will be a time for self-evaluation of the keenest quality, for psychologic adjustment and an attempt to find a pathway to stability. There will be a time when one's judgments may be notably questioned, whether that individual be the health-care professional or the client, but there still should be comfortable and careful cooperation on the part of both. During this time the aim of the evaluator is to be sure that the this client should be considered seriously as a transsexual and the appropriate amount of information is collected and evaluated. Then in time, there will be the appropriate referral to the transition period or real life test.

Whatever length of time it will last, that initial pre-transition evaluation will be a challenge on occasion and the impediments may be frequent. Hopefully, the frustrations will be few. Your scheduled visits will fit a plan designed for all on a general basis but additional evaluative visits will depend upon the presence of added concerns in family, work and social situations. These may have origin in life at a much earlier time or they may be recent concerns. So much will need to be worked through in addition to your gender change plans.

B- The Transition or Real Life Test Period of Time M-F/F-M

The value of this period is that it is an exceedingly good device in the preparation of the transsexual. It is a difficult period for you. It may be viewed as an obstructive and harassing approach and is a very challenging experience, for in it you are asked to present yourself not only to your health-care professional, but to the entire world as a person in the opposite gender. It is a time of measure and worth in readying you as a prospective for eventual surgery. This cannot be stressed enough. The transsexual is asked in this time to live, in every sense of the word, in the role of the crossgendered, to exchange and experience with all in his or her life with family, friends, workplace associates, store clerks, everyone -- as a member of the opposite gender. There should be no escape from this, no tampering with this, no alteration with what this period of time demands. It is a "trial by fire". It is a time of preparation and adjustment. It is not to be taken lightly by patient or counselor. It is in my view, a must!

Some health-care professionals will require only a year. Others ask for two years and even a small number demand as much as five years for this transition period before approval for surgery is granted. Your evaluator may have been the very same person who worked with you in the pre-transition time. On that basis, they certainly will be very knowledgeable as to who you are and what you are experiencing in your life. You will give to them a wealth of personal information and you will be asked to justify your thinking about yourself and your gender identity on numerous occasions.

For those who will attend a gender or identity clinic, there will be an advantage, I believe. All of your team will be there, in one place, for you at various phases of your transitional time. For those who do not have that kind of system to work in, you hopefully will have expert assistance but your team will be separated and there will be a need for you to be certain that there is always appropriate and timely exchange of information between the various professionals who care for you.

Records and data must be exchanged and must be discussed with you. In my experience, doctors don't talk to doctors. Make certain that letters are written, that laboratory data is given to all involved in your care and that progress is assessed and made known to all. There is no excuse for not having this kind of interchange.

Keep in mind also that the transition time will be a time for self evaluation of the keenest quality for psychologic adjustment and to establish and clear a pathway to stability. It will also be a time when one's physical health should be carefully and completely reviewed and reviewed again, for such tampering with biologic sex can be for a few, hazardous and more. This is not a time for game playing but for serious and cooperative interchange.

Keep in mind also that what your friends have experienced may not be relative to you. Their past life experiences are not yours. Their solutions will not match yours even if the problems seem to be the same. Don't make this mistake. You are your own person. Your problems and needs will not be the same. Offer a cooperative and agreeable attitude to your evaluator. That person is acting in a very responsible manner in order to be sure that you really are in the right place in your desires and planning. That professional is not your enemy even when you feel that this might be so. Your professional's knowledge and experience is combined to help ultimately, not to hinder.

Once a reasonable amount of information giving and evaluating takes place, the task of evaluation and planning is put into motion and transition then moves along quite smoothly. Emotional and psychologic baggage will need to be unpacked and perhaps put away or packed once again. Problems dealing with a marriage, with family, the job, all need to be looked at closely and planned for.

How long does it take? How much can you solve yourself or have you worked through before you began this journey? How much will extend over and into your transitional phase? That's what makes you unique, and not the same as your friends moving along next to you. Your mental health-care professional will help you to find the solutions and fashions the tools to prepare yourself for this odyssey.

There is no way to adequately define the length of time it will take you to work through your pre-transitional evaluation and into transition. There is no doubt, however, that once all of the important data has been exchanged between the two of you and you have moved well into transition, this will be a time for your steady progress. Hopefully, there should be an exchange of good experiences or at least a time wherein if problems have arisen that they can be solved very effectively by you and your mental health-care professional together.

As you embark upon this particular phase of time, mentally you should be in the exact and proper place for all that is before you. There may be some mild apprehension, but there should not be fear. There may be some mild anxieties, but there should not be hesitancy. By and large your challenges should not come from your mental health-care professional. The greatest part of that experience should be over with. Your challenges should come from the outside world.

In the case of the M-F, during your pre-transitional evaluation you should have already begun electrolysis. It can be a very difficult problem when asked to live on a full-time basis with a beard. You need much more makeup and you will look quite unnatural. Actually, early in the pre-transitional evaluative phase your counselor should have brought up the discussion with you as to whether or not electrolysis is a favorable step to take. The F-M will not have this kind of problem. Actually, this individual wants very much to have hair growth, but this will not be accomplished for them until hormonal therapy is begun and has continued for a time.

First Impressions - Yours and Theirs M-F/F-M

From the very beginning, from your very first visit to your counselor, and all visits thereafter, you will be assessed at how you conduct yourself, how you look, how you are dressed. Are you flamboyant in your appearance, do you have bizarre makeup or arrangement of clothing, is your whole approach to daily dress bizarre, is your ornamentation out of keeping with what would be practical for that particular time of day? It is very important that you present yourself for the occasion and in a very realistic way. Does this mean a measure of conformity? In a sense, yes it does.

Keep in mind always you are preparing to enter the real world if you are not already in it. Erotic dress, unreal costumes, poor makeup technique and hair management can classify you as one filled with fantasy and not ready to mix with everyday people and events. It is to your great advantage to learn fashion, comportment and to appear as completely as is possible as the opposite gender. Even if you don't "pass", your knowledgeable attempt to be that gender goes to your credit not only in your profession but with all those who are in contact with you. For the M-F electrolysis is exceedingly important. You need less and less makeup with more and more electrolytic treatment. For the F-M individual, binding your breasts and de-emphasizing the female torso is a great benefit. For both the F-M and M-F attention to sitting, standing, walking, gesturing -- all these must be relearned to match the gender you are joining. This attention to detail will be positively noticed by your counselor.

Because of past experiences with transgendered individuals, your mental health-care professional will be critical and perhaps confrontative in your very first visit and for several thereafter. You will, because others have exhibited unacceptable kinds of behavior, come to be suspect of personality traits that won't work in this process. Demanding, manipulative and histrionic approaches will be evident quickly and the result will be a wall built between you and your counselor. Don't do it. You want rapport, cooperation, trust and assistance. That will come only when you prove yourself to be sincere and show evidence of becoming convinced of your pathway. Yes, sincerity and conviction are most important. Believe me, this is the attitude you want to assume and not for the moment, but for all times.

Your counselor will look always for personality problems, such as depression, anti-social attitudes and passive-aggressive disorders. If they are there, they must be addressed and relieved. If not, it will be evidenced soon that they don't exist and you can get on with what you desire most, the solutions to your gender identity conflict.

The Psychologic Evaluation
M-F/F-M

Your psychosocial history will be intensely evaluated in your early exchanges with your mental health-care professional. This begins in the pre-transition time, prior to the real life testing period and it will be ongoing with "revisits" to whatever you have revealed and exchanged on previous occasions. Expect your counselor to delve deeply, to redigest, to recall and to reexamine. Don't resist or lose faith. It's all necessary for your proper placement in the scheme of things. You should know that part of the history taking will be a thorough discussion of sexual habits and fantasies and in addition, an in-depth discussion of any substance abuse particularly alcohol. You will be asked about depression and thoughts about suicide and any attempts at suicide. Tell the truth no matter how you want to suppress or forget. Don't avoid or conceal. You want to come out of this evaluative experience a whole person with preparation and strength to live a fulfilled, happy life as a transgendered person. This is the opportunity to solve problems as nearly as is possible or at least learn how to face them while pursuing your gender conflicts and to prepare for the life that will come thereafter.

Your relationships with family, with friends and the workplace will be an important part of your discussions. What are you trained to do? Can you continue in this area of work in the transition time and after surgery? If not, how can you prepare for another job or vocation? Is school a possibility or a probability to insure a good income and a productive life? It will be extremely important to explore these areas and social service assistance may be brought in to help in the assessment. And what of family? How prepared are you to continue in their lives and they in yours? Are you willing in this crossgendered change to lose all, your parents, your friends and your children? How can you act to avoid that? How can you become a "therapist" of a sort on your own behalf to your family and to your friends?

Be prepared for the probable request to have the counselor interview with family members and a spouse. This may take place in your presence or it may take place often without you being in attendance. A lot of issues and a great deal of confirmation of diagnosis may come from these kinds of interviews. Try not to be resistant or resentful of this and do avoid the temptation to coach these individuals. This will be spotted quickly by your professional. Know also that you may need to prove that you are really cross-living once you are in the transition period. After all, if you are not cross-living who do you fool but yourself? This is a time to rearrange your life, to adjust and to build for the life after surgery. Be honest with yourself, then it is easy to be honest with your professional. If you aren't playing it straight - who do you hurt the most - yourself!

Be prepared for the possibility of referral for a more in-depth type of evaluation with a specialized psychologist or psychiatrist. Some problems may interfere with progression to gender role change for a period of time and must be fully explored or may in time be found to be a contraindication to continuing the crossgender pathway. That is regrettable, but it is the task of mental health-care professionals managing you, to evaluate you as thoroughly and completely as is possible. You must be the ideal candidate or as close to that as is possible for the medical therapy and surgery you anticipate. These professionals have an obligation to direct you correctly. You have an obligation to yourself to cooperate and to look thoroughly at yourself. Does this mean you have no options, no recourse, no opportunity for other opinions? Not at all - it is not intended to be a battle or a struggle. The psychologic evaluation -- is a plan to help gender-conflicted individuals find themselves, help themselves and assist themselves for their future.

If a patient or client is judged to be on a correct pathway and is considered to be one whose progress will likely be smooth and moderate, then in time that patient will be a candidate for medical and laboratory evaluation preparatory to hormonal therapy. If there are some difficulties or problems that need to be worked through, then the transition time may be prolonged and there may be even a delay in the institution of hormonal therapy. Some professionals will recommend hormonal therapy very early in the transition time, for they have the belief that this also helps to treat the individual's dysphoria as well as bring about some measure of physical change in order to make the transition time smoother. Other professionals don't quite follow that line of thinking and pre-fer to hold hormonal therapy for a moderate period of time, perhaps for a year into the transition or real life test period. In their experience, they know of individuals who in real life testing become aware that they are not candidates for continuance and therefore drop out. This eliminates also chance of irre-versible alterations taking place too early in this critical time. Keep in mind, this attitude varies from one professional to another, and there may be reason for strong discussion about this at sometime in your pre-evaluative period or early in your transition, to learn what their view may be.

It would seem that the most experienced and capable mental health-care pro-fessional is one who with a mountain of information can expertly evaluate the preoperative transsexual and sift through the vast complex of gender and psy-chological concerns so as to determine whether this individual is a proper can-didate for contra-gender medical and surgical therapy. The rest of the man-date for the professional is to project with as much accuracy as possible that this person will be stable and adjusted in the life thereafter or have the expected and significant improvement in psychologic and social status. It is a very big task for you both.

The Medical Evaluation
M-F/F-M

Some individuals will already be on hormonal therapy when they come for their initial psychologic evaluations. They may have used them for a short or long time. They may be using their medication correctly or incorrectly. They may not have been evaluated properly for their hormonal regimen or even monitored as is needed while on it. They may be advised to stop. They may not have listened.

It is important that you inform your professional of all the medication you use. Whether it be for specific health problems not related to gender or whether it be a hormonal regimen, you should not conceal those important pieces of information. If you are on hormones and don't declare it, it will be apparent in the baseline laboratory tests your doctor will order for you. It isn't worth the deception. By ordering serum hormone tests for testosterone, luteinizing hormone and follicle-stimulating hormone (the last two are pituitary gonadotrophins), your doctor will know how you make these hormones or if you take them. As baselines they will help to learn in the future how well your eventual hormonal regimen is working on your behalf.

You should know that hormonal levels for appropriate gender, (that is for genetic males - testosterone and for genetic females - estrogen) are invariably normal unless we are dealing with very rare problems of testicular or ovarian failure, either primary or secondary. Inter-sexual problems such as pseudohermaphroditism or Kleinfelter's syndrome are very uncommon as well and will generally be diagnosed quite early in life. This raises the thought as to whether chromosomal analysis need be done when evaluating the transsexual. By and large it would seem unnecessary, but there is one notable exception. The genotype of 47 XXY (Kleinfelter's) can rarely be found in individuals with no clinical stigmata of the disorder. By that I mean, they have none of the typical physical appearances of other individuals having Kleinfelter's with that chromosomal alteration.

This raises an important point. Kleinfelter (M-F) individuals have an incidence of breast cancer similar to genetic females. Dr. Kleinfelter himself reports an incidence of breast cancer twenty (20) times greater in his patients with this chromosomal abnormality than in normal genotype males who are 46 XY. This could be a potential problem for the transgendered Kleinfelter individual taking estrogen, and while there are no reports as yet in the medical literature, this situation is something to be aware of and to advise such a patient about. While we are considering this question of breast cancer in genetic males who are 46

XY and taking estrogen, you should feel comfortable with the fact that there are only three reported cases of breast cancer in this population as found in the medical literature over the last twenty years to reassure you this is not a concern, but the proper study has not yet been done to know whether individuals in larger assessment groups might be at greater risk. There are other medical concerns to be made aware of when genetic males use estrogen and genetic females use testosterone and we will look at these considerations in detail.

The Evaluation of the Transsexual About to Take Hormonal Therapy M-F/F-M

We shall consider the initial evaluation of the genetic male and genetic female, the baseline studies to be done at the time that hormonal therapy is being planned, and then the monitoring or follow up schedule will be outlined. Keep in mind physicians will do things differently. Some will order testing not always necessary in order to be certain that **all** is going well. Others might not order quite enough and this will not always be to your advantage. Some may prescribe one regimen of hormonal therapy while others have another plan that has worked well for them and their patients. The cardinal rule for you to remember is that **moderate amounts of medication over time with proper monitoring will produce all the changes the transsexual individual will be capable of accomplishing due to their own individual tissue response**. Expectations must always be realistic. Fantasy is not a part of medical therapy. The transsexual on hormones may respond differently then someone they know taking the exact same regimen. Your doctor is aware of this and there is no certain way to predict just what your responses will be. There may be room for modification of a regimen in order to produce something more in the way of physical results. However, even with those modifications only just so much can be expected.

History Taking M-F/F-M

Your physician will want to know all of the details of health and disease in your family. What you can remember about health habits, the development of illness and the mode of death of all members of your family is all important for you in your medical evaluation. A history of cardiovascular disease, of blood pressure elevation, a diabetic family history or cancer history in certain members of the family --- all of this has an impact upon you. You don't always necessarily inherit the tendency for these disorders, but it's vital to tell your physician what your family experienced. It is a very important part of your medical history.

Your own personal and surgical history will be evaluated as well and your ability to supply appropriate information about illness and the degree of recovery as well as the use of medications is very important. You should be prepared to obtain records of hospitalizations and their outcome. You are wise to prepare some of this information beforehand, for you will be asked this at some time in the near future. Part of your physician's inquiry will include a sexual history and an in-depth discussion of alcohol, and tobacco use. Any drug or other substance abuse history is important to disclose.

For the F-M individual, a complete gynecologic history is very important. An inquiry will be made about menses and gynecologic infection in the past. It is essential that knowledge about your obstetrical experiences in the past be shared with your physician, as well.

Assessment of Psychologic Status M-F/F-M

While the greatest part of your psychosocial status is the task of your mental health-care professional, there are times when you see your medical physician that you may present with certain experiences or feelings that will be very important to make known to your doctor. He or she should be making evaluations of how you appear, how you feel emotionally and what you have experienced in the way of stress since your last visit. Keeping record of these events is important since that information should be transmitted to your mental health-care professional and added to the growing fund of data in your evaluation.

Your doctor does not need to go in depth with these evaluations, but some assessment of how you are managing on a daily basis is very important.

The Baseline Physical Examination of the Male-to-Female Individual - M-F

This should be done in a most thorough manner from head to toe. The ears, eye and eye grounds (funduscopic exam) must be evaluated along with the facial glands (salivary and lymph nodes). The thyroid and tracheal area, the mouth and it's structures and dentition should be examined and recorded.

The chest must be examined very thoroughly for skeletal defect and any breast development should be noted and measured (hemi-circumference). A careful examination of the heart and lungs is essential and then the abdomen is examined. Palpation is to be done to check for enlarged organs or masses.

Hips, waist and buttocks area should be measured and recorded for later comparisons.

Is there evidence of inguinal herniation, actual or expected? Are the testes both in the scrotum and are they normal and equal in size? They can and should be measured. (An urologist has means for doing this that should be known to all physicians.) A rectal exam is needed for any unusual enlargements, for evidence of infection and for evaluation of the prostate.

The legs are examined for varicose veins and vein competency and some inquiry should be made about periodic edema or fluid retention in this area. The lower extremity pulses are felt and compared and some inspection of the feet, hands and nails is important to record.

The skin is an organ unto itself as well as a reflection of disorders within the body. It should be looked at carefully and this includes arms, legs and trunk, front and back. Some record of muscle strength and appearance is important. Height and posture should also be observed and recorded along with weight and pulse, respiratory rate and blood pressure, the latter while sitting and lying down.

A moderately thorough neurologic examination, including evaluation of the cranial nerves and the peripheral nervous system will be very important for the physician to conduct.

In short, this entire baseline examination is done to assess one's overall physical status and level of health in preparation for hormonal use. Your physician is charged with not just the prescription of gender hormones but with the assessment of good health or lack of it. If changes take place brought about by the hormonal regimen to be instituted, then comparison with these baseline evaluations can be very meaningful.

Follow up visits for monitoring of one's physical health and progress on hormonal therapy will be scheduled on the basis of what your physician believes necessary for appropriate monitoring. Those visits may be every three to four months during the first year and should be extended to perhaps once every six months thereafter until surgery is completed, depending upon your physical health and the data that is sent to your doctor from the laboratory. Your physician's careful inquiry should pinpoint certain areas that are not comfortable for you in the use of your hormonal regimen and evaluations should be directed towards those complaints. Your physician's inquiry should include questions that search for emotional change, depression or any disturbance in your psychosocial stability. Discussion of diet, weight control and a review of your smoking and alcohol use is a part of that inquiry as well.

Subsequent physical examinations need not be as exhaustive as it was in the very first examination. In addition to evaluation of your heart, lungs, abdomen and legs for varicose vein development and fluid retention, (edema) there should also be appropriate evaluation and measurement of your breasts, of your hips and waist and derriere. Your blood pressure and weight should be recorded as well. Once a year, it will be appropriate to evaluate the prostate gland by way of a rectal exam as well. Monitoring of your physical health status can be done very efficiently and over a very short period of time with a specific plan that your physician should follow very carefully. Eventually, all of this data will be placed in the hands of your operating surgeon and a very careful review of your progress during that transition time will be important for the exchange to come between you and your operating surgeon.

The Baseline Physical Examination of the Female-to Male - F-M

This physical examination should include all that is needed to establish good health and physical status. It must be thorough and all inclusive.

To begin with, your weight, height and blood pressure must be recorded. Examination of the head and neck includes the eyes, ears and mouth for any deviation or abnormality. Dentition must be adequate and in good health and a presence of salivary gland and lymph node enlargement is to be noted. The thyroid gland is to be felt. The chest examination in next with attention to the heart, lungs and breasts. A very careful examination of the breasts is essential and you should be taught how to do self-breast examination in the correct manner. The abdomen is palpated for liver size and to be certain that no other enlargements exist. The extremities are examined to detect fluid retention and the presence of vein enlargement and/or evidence of vein incompetency. The arterial pulses in the groin, behind the knees and on the top of the foot are felt and compared. Attention to the presence of any skeletal deformity and some assessment of muscle strength is important and the skin is evaluated carefully both on the trunk and the extremities. The skin is an organ susceptible to its own disorders and alterations but it is also a part of other kinds of internal disease and should be evaluated for these possibilities.

A rectal and pelvic examination is all important. It must be thorough and done by someone who is experienced in conducting this type of examination. Pelvic enlargements and infections must be ruled out completely. A pap smear must be done at this time and should be done periodically thereafter. Lastly, a fairly complete neurologic evaluation is a part of this physical exam. Evaluation of the cranial and peripheral nerve system is to be done along with inspection of the eye grounds or the retina of the eye (funduscopic).

Subsequent examinations or monitoring visits can be shorter and less intensive and they are scheduled as your physician believes it important for your evaluation depending upon your status of health and your reaction to your hormonal regimen. Certainly attention must be directed to weight, blood pressure determinations (sitting and lying down), along with evaluation of the skin and special focus is given to hair growth and clitoral growth. Evaluations made along with measurements and recording of these areas of progress is essential. Inquiry as to menstrual function is all important. On an effective hormonal regimen F-M individuals will lose menstrual function within months. There will be voice changes evident in the first six months of therapy but real in-depth changes in pitch may take as much as a year or so to become evident. This is a non-reversible change. Varying amounts of extremity and facial hair growth can be expected in five to six months of hormonal use and clitoral growth will be evident certainly within that six month period as well. These are also non-reversible changes.

In subsequent visits, your physician's careful inquiry should pinpoint certain areas that are not comfortable in the use of your hormonal regimen and evaluation should be directed towards those complaints. Your physician's inquiry should include questions that search for emotional change, depression or any disturbance in your psychosocial stability. Discussion of diet, weight control and a review of your smoking and alcohol use is a part of that inquiry as well.

A monitoring of your physical health status can be done very efficiently and over a very short period of time with a specific plan that your physician should follow very carefully. Eventually all of this data will be placed in the hands of your operating surgeon. A very careful review of your progress during that transition time will be important for the exchange between you and that operating surgeon when surgery is planned.

Laboratory Evaluation During the Transition - M-F/F-M

Baseline laboratory evaluations are important to you and your physician as well. Your doctor may consider not only routine chemistries and counts to be assured of your overall good health but look at certain specific tests and use of them as guides to the appropriateness of your hormonal regimen.

The **routine** studies that all individuals should have periodically include some system studies that can be altered by hormonal use. The following are the minimum to be done to be sure that all is in good order, both in your overall health and in changes that are being brought about by your hormonal regimen:

a. A CBC (complete blood count) with a differential is a test to be sure that the cells in the bloodstream are in right amounts and ratios. This determines, for instance, if anemia is present and when serum platelets are evaluated, their count tells your physician a little about the tendency to bleeding disorders. The CBC is very important to the F-M individual because a few in this population develop polycythemia. This is an excess of red blood cells that takes place when some individuals use testosterone and should be noted if it is taking place.

b. The BUN (blood urea nitrogen), creatinine and uric acid tests give some information about kidney function. They are routine and helpful to assure that these organs are functioning correctly.

c. The liver is an organ that performs a great number of tasks in our bodies and while some of the tests for liver function indicate only a small amount of what is happening in that organ, the following are done on a routine basis and can give indication that all is working correctly. Your doctor may ask for serum proteins which include albumin and globulin. He/she may ask for bilirubin testing and may ask for a test that evaluates the enzyme, alkaline phosphatase. SGOT and SGPT are enzymes measuring liver function as well and these can be altered when one is taking hormones. Abnormal results will point to a need to perform other liver function studies and perhaps alter the hormonal regimen. This area of testing is most important to both the F-M and the M-F individual and your physician should always be looking at tests that involve liver function.

d. T3, T4, TSH are special studies of thyroid activity and when the thyroid is malfunctioning, these will be altered. This can take place while using estrogen medication. Occasional individuals develop under-active thyroid function or have a worsening of an already existing hypothyroidism, and testing here is very important for the M-F individual.

e. Calcium and phosphorus tests may help to discover any alteration that could give insight into changes in bone metabolism or tendencies of other diseases that affect the levels of calcium and phosphorus in our blood. These would be important tests also in individuals who have a tendency for developing stones in the gall bladder or in the kidneys.

f. Electrolyte balance is a very important function in our bodies and intimately involved with water metabolism. Measurements of potassium and sodium give indication of proper function in certain systems and these electrolytes can be influenced by a feminization program, for example when using anti-androgens, such as spironolactone (Aldactone).

g. The lipid profile which includes serum cholesterol, triglycerides, LDL and HDL are very important to monitor in all individuals at various times in life, but certainly those individuals who are on hormonal regimens need this set of tests especially. I emphasize that the F-M transsexual have these tests done often.

h. For older M-F individuals, a PSA test should be done at various times. This is a screening test to rule out the potential of prostatic cancer. The likelihood of this developing in the M-F on an estrogen program may be small, but nonetheless, it should be done yearly.

Special Laboratory Tests - M-F/F-M

There are special studies that may help to monitor the changes that take place in a person on a hormone regimen. These include the following:

a. Luteinizing hormones and follicle-stimulating hormone --- These are hormones which come from the pituitary gland. They are known as gonadotropins and they are used to help assess the amount of estrogen or testosterone that is circulating in the bloodstream.

b. Estrogen determinations - These may be done to assist in evaluating the levels of estrogen in the bloodstream. This, of course, will be elevated in the M-F transsexual on estrogens and may give good indication as to whether or not the individual is within the genetic female limits. It is not, however, a test that needs to be repeated very frequently.

c. Testosterone determinations - These are perhaps much more helpful in guiding the physician as to whether or not the hormonal regimen is adequate. If your level of testosterone as a M-F transsexual comes within the genetic female range, you are being very adequately treated with hormones. For the F-M individual, it may be important to measure serum testosterone from time to time to see how efficiently it is suppressing circulating estrogen levels. However, the physical appearance of the F-M is usually the most noteworthy guide as to the effectiveness of the regimen.

d. Prolactin determinations - This is a hormone that is found in the genetic male as well as the genetic female. It comes from the pituitary gland and it is always affected and elevated by estrogen use. For a **very few** M-F individuals, the elevation is inordinately high and this must be evaluated on a periodic basis, generally much more frequently in the first year of estrogen use. If this substance is found to be too high in the M-F, it will be important to interrupt the estrogen therapy and assess the levels of prolactin once estrogen has been discontinued. If this elevation persists, then the individual must be studied. It could imply the beginning of pituitary changes that are associated with a growth or tumor. This is quite uncommon and you must not be afraid of this in the use of your medication. However, your doctor should be aware of the importance of this periodic laboratory determination.

Additional Tests and Procedures - M-F/F-M

In the course of your initial evaluation or in subsequent visits, your physician may find reason to order testing and procedures in addition to the usual and standard kinds of laboratory tests. Many of these, I am sure, you have heard of and are somewhat acquainted with, but to give you a more in-depth idea of what some of these are about and why they are conducted, is important. Of course as with other aspects of your medical health and your medication regimen, discussion with your physician is all important and it is always to your advantage to ask what the procedure is for, and what you can expect when you go to the hospital or laboratory for the study. When that study has been done and the results reported to your physician, you should expect a report and discussion about the information that has been sent to him or her.

The MRI (Magnetic Resonance Imaging) - This is a type of scan that can yield a great deal more information than other forms of scanning. This is not to say that the MRI is the very best of techniques for looking into our bodies and reviewing certain areas and systems. In very experienced hands this can give a great deal of important information. MRI's can be used in orthopedic problems as well as afflictions and concerns affecting the central nervous system, and disorders in the organs within the chest and abdomen. The MRI technique has been expanded such that it can be utilized for many different kinds of problems and complaints.

When looking at the cardiovascular system, the heart and blood vessels, a great number of techniques and procedures have been developed. You likely are acquainted with the standard EKG (electrocardiogram) and depending upon your age and your past medical history and findings at any one physical examination, it may be necessary to secure a baseline EKG for comparison at later times.

If there is indication on the basis of physical findings or complaint, you may be asked to have much more sophisticated types of electrocardiography. Vector electrocardiography is one of those kinds of testing. Sometimes thallium stress tests are asked for in order to see how your heart responds to imposed activity, under certain conditions. Angiography may be a part of the studies ordered for you. This is a technique utilizing radiopaque dye that is placed in the various arteries of our body. The arterial circulation of the heart, of the brain and even peripheral vasculature can be studied by this technique.

Leg Blood Vessel Studies - In addition to using angiography for outlining the arteries of the lower extremities, there are also tests that can be applied to study the competency of your veins in this area. Venography - a procedure which utilizes radiopaque dye and Doppler Studies - a method of ultrasound can be used to determine competency of the veins and to determine whether or not there may be some inflammatory change (phlebitis) or obstruction with a clot (thrombosis). Phlebitis and clot formation can lead to the passage of a clot from the leg veins into the lungs (embolism). This can be a very serious sequence and, on occasion, it can lead to death. Hence, the assurance that veins are healthy through these various evaluations is highly important.

The gastrointestinal tract can be studied in a variety of ways. Barium swallows for outlining the esophagus, the stomach and the small bowel can be a part of the regimen used to study some of your complaints. Barium instillation can be utilized for looking at the large bowel. Various kinds of visual procedures (endoscopy) help also to look at the interior of these structures. Colonoscopy is a technique used to study the large bowel with complaints of indigestion and pain, and a technique known as gastroscopy can provide vision into the esophagus, the entire stomach and a measure of the small bowel depending upon special complaints or a particular family history. A proctoscope may be used to look at the interior of the lower large bowel.

Sonography - This technique, also known as ultrasound, can be used to visualize the gall bladder area, the liver and may at times be used to clarify certain findings in the breasts. Sonar can be applied to a number of other areas and systems of our body, for instance, growths or tumors in the pelvic region, or the kidneys, can be visualized by this technique.

There are a large number of other kinds of studies that give information. Simple x-rays of the chest and of the abdomen are often times helpful to determine cause or complaint. Your physician may at times feel the need for ordering mammography to determine whether or not there are any growths in the breast, or to help to determine the nature of something that is felt in one or both breasts. Intravenous pyelograms (IVP) may be ordered because of complaints in the upper or lower urinary tract. Various kinds of pathology such as stones, tumor and kidney malfunction can be diagnosed more effectively by the use of ultrasound and IVP's. Sometimes a cystoscopic examination is necessary. This is visualization of the interior of the bladder and urethra with a special instrument called a cystoscope.

Medical science has come a very long way in the ability to learn more and more about our body and its function. These are just a few of the tests that perhaps you may have contact with depending upon certain aspects of health. Certain complaints that you may bring to your physician through your evaluation and monitoring and in life thereafter may bring you in contact with some of these studies.

When can you expect to begin your Hormonal Regimen? - M-F/F-M

Your health-care professional whether a psychologist, a psychiatrist or internal medical physician, and whether they are acting alone or in concert with a gender team, may have fixed views as to when hormones should be started. Some professionals believe that hormones should be started early in the real life test period. They feel, as did the transgender medicine pioneer, Dr. Harry Benjamin, some years ago that there is therapeutic value to their use and that even early, physical change no matter how slight, can be a distinct psychologic aid to the transsexual in their transitional time. They believe as well that there is a diagnostic value to the use of hormones in the very early phases of the transition. Some individuals who are not comfortable with the feelings and the physical alterations will then self-diagnose and eliminate themselves from a transsexual program.

Other professionals, however, will be reluctant to use this approach. They feel that more time is needed to evaluate and eventually clarify and hopefully solve other issues. They feel that it is important to wait quite a bit more time to solidify the diagnosis and to solve other problems. They fear also, particularly in the case of the F-M individual that irreversible changes may take place and with inadequate preparation or with withdrawal from such a program for whatever reasons, the individual may have created for themselves, far more problems than they had at the very beginning. Hence, this group of professionals will delay hormones until well into the real life test.

The transsexual doesn't benefit altogether by this, yet the fear is great that with loss of purpose, interest or candidacy on the part of the transsexual, nothing irreversible is begun. There is room to discuss either attitude. Generally, I believe the decision for the start of hormones should be made on an individual basis. Some patients will be clearly candidates for medication early in their evaluation. Others may demonstrate the need to delay, but reassessments should be appropriate and open for discussion.

The Hormonal Regimen for the Male-to-Female - M-F

There is no uniformity as yet in the medical literature as to the kind of medications or the dosage to be used. In theory, the best regimen I believe is an estrogen in moderate dosage in combination with an anti-androgen. For example, an initial or starting dose of Premarin 2.5 mg. or Estinyl 0.05 mg. daily along with 100 mg. of spironolactone would be quite appropriate for two to three months. If tolerated well and all evaluations at that interval seemed to be in good order, then moving the Premarin up to 5.0 mg. each day or using Estinyl to 0.5 mg daily along with an increase of spironolactone to 200 mg. per day would be a reasonable approach. Increments in estrogen should not be considered for another six months but spironolactone could be increased by 100 mg. each three month visit up to 400 mg. if no problem is encountered.

The guidelines your physician will consider will be **your** sense of wellness and well-being, and **your** gradual, but definite, physical alteration and stability in your laboratory studies. He or she should evaluate your liver enzymes, your lipid profiles, thyroid studies, prolactin levels and a gradual decrease of your serum testosterone to genetic female levels.

Is there room for other regimens? Yes, there is and there are a number of them reported in the medical literature. Some physicians use injectable estrogen to supplement the oral estrogen regimen. Others will use a product called Lupron, an injectable long-acting anti-androgen lasting a month and requiring more frequent visits for the medication.

I do not endorse any specific approach, but I do emphasize the need for moderation, for careful monitoring and for patience. This formula works over time.

Preliminary reporting is in the medical literature about the use of a skin patch - Estraderm. The recommendations are principally two in number.

    a. It should be used in the hormonal regimens of all M-F individuals above the age of 40 years, either pre or postoperative. It accomplishes very adequate physical change in combination with an antiandrogen.

    b. It can be used in M-F individuals whose regimen of estrogen use has been interrupted because of the complication of phlebitis and/or embolism (blood clot to the lungs). A series of post phlebitic individuals have been studied and followed with use of the topical Estraderm patch, and none have had recurrent vein or blood clot problems. Heretofore this group would never be permitted estrogen again. With the skin patch, their regimen can be reinstituted.

Expectations for the Male to Female on Hormones - M-F

Breasts - A 10 cm. increase in size could be expected in the first year of a hormonal regimen. The hemi-circumference of the breast should be measured at each doctor's visit and recorded. In the next year, perhaps an increase of 8-10 cm. could be expected with appropriate change in the areola appearance and size. The nipple, however, does not change very much. In general, growth for most may be just a little less than that in the genetic female. Sensitivity and tenderness will be intermittent and variable. All patients should wait for about two years of therapy to pass before considering any breast augmentation procedures. Once again, it is tissue response that is important and not all individuals will have comparable growth, even when using the same regimen.

Early in treatment, just behind the nipple, there will be changes that could mimic a small tumor. Don't be worried about this. This has to do with increase in the ductal system behind the nipple.

Skin - The skin becomes smoother and softer and if the patient has had electrolysis for facial hair, the skin there will be very velvety.

Fat distribution - Gradually, there will be a change in subcutaneous fat distribution. More deposition will be evident on the hips and on the derriere. The waist does not change, hence the narrow waistline of the female is not going to result. Measurements of the waist, hips and fanny area should be made with your doctor visits to demonstrate this slow but distinct alteration. Continued measurements of the hip/waist ratio will be noticeable, though change is very gradual.

Genitalia - Generally, there is some shortening of the penis and while some authors in the medical literature state that this does not happen, it is definitely evident in some individuals. It does have importance later when the M-F individual is a candidate for surgery. Penile length is directly proportional to the creation of the vagina and it's length. It will have some importance in the selection of the type of procedure the surgeon will use in the reassignment surgery.

The individual's testes will diminish in size and in volume. Histologic studies reported in the literature indicate definite changes are evident in certain cellular elements. Those cells that are responsible for production of testosterone and for the development of sperm are severely affected by estrogen use. All of this is evident in the ejaculate, the fluid that comes from the penis with sexual relations. The volume of the ejaculate is also notably reduced and may even at times be negligible or absent. This happens because of estrogen's effect upon the prostate and other structures that are responsible for the producing this fluid.

The testes can be measured. Urologists have a technique using wooden or plastic ovoids to make size comparison with the testes and the size of your testes and penis should be measured as well with selected visits.

Prostate gland - As mentioned before, the prostate gland is reduced in size and older M-F individuals who have some urinary complaints because of benign prostatic enlargement prior to the use of estrogen will report improvement once estrogen is begun. When they take estrogenic medication, the start of urination is easier and the caliber of the urinary stream is increased. Dribbling due to sphincter incompetency may not totally disappear but can improve considerably. Your doctor should be doing rectal exams periodically and still obtaining a special blood test called PSA. While there is a strong suspicion that estrogen can be protective to the prostate from the standpoint of cancer development, we still need a study that hopefully will be done one day showing the prophylactic value of estrogen against not only malignant but benign disease.

Lipid profile - Serum cholesterol, triglycerides, and the lipoproteins substances LDL and HDL, which transport cholesterol in the blood, are all part of the lipid profile. By and large, testing of this sort should indicate that the M-F person benefits as does the genetic female taking estrogen. All other influences on cholesterol from diet, exercise, genetic influence and smoking habits are still important factors to be considered. Estrogen cannot be expected to do it all for the M-F person, but it can be of great help in reducing arteriosclerotic plaque disease and delaying cardiovascular incidents.

Now let us consider what things estrogen certainly will not do:

Often the M-F transsexual fantasizes a beautiful female figure and a lovely lilting feminine voice, both resulting from hormone use. Be assured, neither will happen. The waist, as I mentioned earlier, does not become narrower but rather stays the same or may even increase due to weight gain. The vocal cords once altered by testosterone production in the pubertal years will not change, hence the deep masculine voice remains.

At one time in the past false rib removal was done to provide a narrower waist. I have seen two individuals who had such surgery and the results were quite striking, but I am aware of no surgeon who currently performs this procedure for the M-F individual. Voice box surgery and/or vocal training will be needed to alter voice pitch. A voice therapist can be very helpful. Ultimately, voice pitch surgery while it carries notable success for some, along with some failure rate for others, can be extremely helpful for the M-F individual. Sometimes the two approaches are necessary together.

Potential problems and complications for the Male to Female - M-F

Weight gain - Most individuals will experience some increase in their weight. Counseling and instruction as to how to shop for food, its preparation and calorie counting will be very necessary. For some, a dietician in consultation may be needed. I am not referring to problems of fluid retention. That is a likelihood as well, but overweight if it exists before hormones are started, implies that eating habits are faulty. The individual will need education and physician watchfulness in subsequent visits. For some, estrogen use and weight reduction or weight maintenance can be a very difficult problem.

Vein problems - Leg pain and fatigue can develop from vein sensitivity and from the accentuation of already incompetent veins (varicose veins) under the influence of estrogen and other hormones, e.g. progesterone. This can be dealt with in a variety of ways. Elevation of the lower extremities at certain times of the day and evening, and supportive hosiery are just two of several approaches. Surgery can be considered to improve the competency of the superficial venous system in the lower extremities. Special surgeons can be consulted for this.

The real problem with hormonal therapy for a certain percentage of users however, is phlebitis (vein inflammation). This may or may not be associated with blood clot to the lungs (embolism). Age and duration of hormone use seem to be important factors in some studies and the statement is made often in several studies that high doses of estrogen in particular, tend to increase the risk for phlebitis. M-F individuals who are under forty have less risk. M-F individuals using their hormones for over a year also have less risk.

In some physician's view, once an individual has developed phlebitis their use of estrogen is most probably at an end. Hence, this is a very serious complication with estrogen use, not only because it is life threatening, but because it means the feminization program is greatly hindered. We mentioned however, recent reporting of use of the Estraderm skin patch.

The incidence of phlebitis in a major study from the Netherlands is a little over 6%. That is notable enough to be on the lookout for such a complication. Your doctor should instruct you about some of the signs to watch for.

Hypertension - This can develop in a few patients or can be accentuated in a few who already have mild hypertension. In the Free University Hospital of Amsterdam study, the incidence of hypertension overall was just under 5% with two thirds of the group newly diagnosed as having elevated blood pressure. All of the fourteen patients reported continued on an estrogen regimen along with appropriate anti-hypertensive therapy and they were managed quite successfully. It would seem that it is a concern to be aware of and to be managed appropriately, but not a contraindication to the use of hormones.

Hypothyroidism - Disorders wherein estrogen is used or produced in excess in genetic women, can often times interfere with thyroid activity, often increasing the size of the gland and its workload. This is evident for instance in the first trimester of pregnancy, and thyroid function studies reflect this as with other states of increased estrogen activity. On occasion, this is the case for the M-F transgendered person as well. The doctor must be alert to this uncommon but definite endocrine alteration, for it is important to diagnose and to treat. Individuals with a thyroid under-activity already in place may need additional thyroid medication once they begin using estrogen.

Pituitary changes - Every M-F individual will have an elevation of the serum prolactin level once starting estrogen. An occasional one will be elevated quite notably and if above a specific level that your doctor will know to watch for, alterations will be necessary in your regimen and some investigation will be proper. If the estrogen is stopped and the prolactin levels decrease to acceptable limits, the estrogen can be reinstituted, although in lower doses, for it is known that the increased prolactin levels may be dose-related. Elevated levels have to do also with age. If prolactin levels remain in acceptable limits, then the revised regimen can be continued and only periodic serum prolactin determinations need be done. If, however, the levels go back beyond the acceptable limit on the lower doses or if without estrogen the levels remain higher than acceptable, then the pituitary gland must be evaluated by scanning techniques. This is very important for it implies growth of the gland or perhaps the development of a tumor, known as a prolactinoma.

One other point to be made is that the anti-androgen, Androcur may also elevate prolactin levels. This must be considered when a regimen of estrogen and Androcur are used in combination.

This is not a common complication but it is reported in the medical literature, and when such concerning prolactin elevations do occur, your doctor must be certain that other factors are not involved.

Stress, exercise programs, alterations in diet, even an under-active thyroid can elevate the serum prolactin. Your doctor will be aware of the fact that collection of blood for testing for serum prolactin must be timed, for prolactin production is at its lowest level, usually in the latter part of the day or in the evening. Prolactin production is known to be pulsatile. By that I mean it has peaks and valleys through a 24-hour period.

Changes in vision may also take place, but often times the serum prolactin levels in the blood are clues to this before that complaint develops. All hormones must be interrupted and medical treatment with special medications may be necessary. If that medical therapy does not produce desired results, there is also a surgical procedure that can be done, but this would not be considered without an appropriate consultation with a neurosurgeon.

Sexual activity - A variety of changes may take place in this area. We have mentioned changes in the penile length and in the size of the testes. These changes alone will influence sexual function. With lower testosterone and lowered, or loss of, sperm development, infertility can take place. Penile erection is possible but it is not a spontaneous activity. Stimulation is necessary and the erection in most instances will not be maintained for long. Libido is decreased measurably. The M-F for a number of reasons but certainly with estrogen use, may be very passive both in sexual performance and appetite. Performance may be short lived and of lesser quality. Those who want to preserve male adequacy in sexual relations may experience change quite considerably and to a point of diminished satisfaction for the sexual partner. Orgasm is still possible but it may have less quality. The whole experience is altered and for the person desiring a regimen for maximal feminization, it should be understood that male sexual activity and satisfaction can be for a great many, altered considerably.

Stone formation - Gall bladder disease as it occurs more commonly in women during the childbearing years becomes more of a reality for the genetic male on estrogen therapy. Some transgendered individuals on hormones feel that their experience with kidney stones has increased on such a regimen as well. There is no reporting in the medical literature to support this latter contention.

Cardiovascular disease - There is no reason to believe that estrogen has any influence on those forms of heart disease that have to do with the heart valves or with heart rhythm, but there is some concern about coronary vessel disease and the worsening of this process when estrogen is used by genetic males. Much of the concern comes from reports in the medical literature of a worsening of heart disease and increased mortality in men treated with estrogens for metastatic prostatic cancer. One point must be kept in mind when reading these studies. Those studied were in a much older group of males with coronary heart disease already in place to a lesser or greater degree. All study candidates were 70 or more years old.

Information about prior cardiac history of patients was not given in any amount of detail in some papers and no special prior cardiac monitoring was done before the institution of the estrogen regimen in other studies. Nor were there any postmortem or autopsy studies accompanying the reporting. Generally, the transgendered population using hormones will be notably younger and in better cardiac health. They will be selected more carefully than the candidates in prostate cancer treatment groups and in appropriate instances they will be evaluated much more closely before hormones are started. Without doubt, older transgendered individuals desiring hormones **must** be evaluated more initially and then monitored with great care as they continue their programs. But reports in the literature of cardiac death in M-F transgendered individuals using estrogen are infrequent. In a study from the Free University Hospital in Amsterdam of over 700 individuals, 9 developed documented myocardial infarctions (a kind of heart attack), with several having died. Usually a strong family history of coronary heart disease is evident and smoking is generally in the patient's daily habits. Patients must be identified as possible risks and then monitored on a regular basis once the regimen is started.

The incidence of this serious complication is not great though nonetheless, very real. Alertness on the part of your physician is mandatory, when dealing with individuals 40 years and older especially. There is every reason to believe however that the same cardio-protective effects of estrogen in the genetic female can be found in the M-F transgendered person on an estrogen regimen.

Emotional health - On a spontaneous basis, transgendered individuals will often disclose what they experience emotionally once they are on hormones. In general, most are quite comfortable and in fact elated. They are finally on a pathway they have wanted to travel for years. They feel wonderful. But some notice a change in their feelings. They have tendency to depression and negativism. How much is attributable to the hormone regimen and how much to other psychosocial alterations in their lives is often hard to evaluate. Nonetheless, there is a distinct number who report such mental changes and the greater number of these lose those feelings in a moderate period of time. This implies that outside stresses and pressures in family, work and peer situations are more a cause than the medication. In addition, personality variables in the patient may play a very definite role. The likelihood is that very little of this can be attributed **solely** to the hormone regimen. Still suicide or attempts to commit suicide are in evidence in the literature and this concerns writers and researchers working in transgendered medical care. I find it hard to indite medication alone however for such emotional instability and self-destructive attempts. I think the transgendered, especially the true transsexual, has so much to cope with in life, trying to find congruence, acceptance and stability that the mental climate for some is extremely troubled.

Liver function studies - A study of liver activity in the M-F individual is all important in the initial use of an estrogen program and it must be looked at periodically thereafter. The liver is such a multi-function organ, that measurements of certain enzymes and substances in the blood seems to be a good screen for evaluating liver integrity and health. A percentage of M-F people have transient adverse alterations in these studies with early use of the estrogen, but most revert to normal studies in a short time. Those with persistent elevations usually have a prior history of liver insult either from infection or alcohol/drug abuse. If these disease states are currently active or if the liver is notably damaged by these entities, then estrogen use can be a further insult and its use must be discontinued, if started at all.

The work of some researchers seems to indicate that a damaged liver does not handle estrogen well. A healthy liver is generally not troubled by estrogen use and handles it well as the estrogen passes through the organ and is catabolized (broken down) there.

Miscellaneous complaints - A number of lesser concerns may be evident as the hormonal regimen continues. Individuals may experience a number of gastrointestinal disorders, nausea, abdominal pain and digestive and elimination problems may develop with estrogen, especially when using oral preparations. Skin rash, localized or generalized, nail brittleness and fluid retention are all occasional complaints. Infrequently, an individual may have problems with glasses requiring periodic examinations or may show inability to wear contact lens because of changes in the front-to-back diameter of the globe of the eye. These annoyances rarely cause such a problem that the estrogen is discontinued and institution of a different regimen can be helpful.

The Hormonal Regimen for the Female-to-Male - F-M

Masculinizing medication seems to be the most efficient by injection for the F-M person. Testosterone esters given every two to four weeks are the approaches most physicians offer. Oral medication is available but not employed as much, for blood levels do not seem to be as uniform and physical results are not as prompt as many individuals would like. Oral preparations have more effect upon liver health. Large quantities are not absorbed from the small bowel and are lost in waste material. Hence not as high blood stream levels as desired are attained.

A skin patch has been developed but may not be appropriate for the F-M in transition. More study is needed to determine its efficiency.

Commonly, testosterone undecanoate, testosterone propionate and testosterone cypionate in 20-40 mg. doses, given every two to four weeks, are the usual products and the results are very rewarding. Changes for the F-M individual on an appropriate hormonal regimens are very much more altering and efficient then for the M-F on estrogen and discussion of these changes will soon follow. Dose regimens are altered depending on several factors:

a. Cessation of menses is a very important goal. On an adequate regimen, 50% of hormone recipients will stop menstruating by three months. Another 40% or more will stop menses by six months of therapy. The remaining few may need adjustment of the injectable dose or have an oral progesterone preparation added to the daily routine to completely stop all remaining uterine activity.

b. Uncomfortable side effects or laboratory changes may prompt the need for altering testosterone medication and these will be discussed in detail in a short while. Meanwhile, distinct physical changes will commence and these changes generally are not reversible. Monitoring of these changes and the individual's feeling of well being while on this regimen along with appropriate blood studies every three months for the first year is most appropriate. Laboratory evaluations of liver function, lipid profile and routine blood cell evaluations are necessary with each of these visits.

Expectations for the Female-to-Male on Hormones - F-M

Before discussing what testosterone will do in the genetic female, let's make mention of several important concepts:

1. We are tampering in a sense with systems that have been in place all through life and especially with the effects of the ovarian hormone, estrogen, which began to create change in the pubertal years.

2. Tissue response and time will bring to the individual virtually all that is to be accomplished for that individual. There is no shortcut to alteration of physical characteristics.

3. Administration of testosterone for the F-M individual can be by mouth, but intramuscular injection is a better route. Liver involvement is lessened somewhat this way, and more importantly, the effects are much more pronounced.

Now in the genetic female, the positive responses to testosterone are these:

Menstrual function - On an adequate regimen, half of those taking the hormone will have no more menses within three months. Most of the remaining half will lose all menstrual function with six months of use. A small number will have some menstrual activity or intermittent spotting and require alterations in dosage or addition of an oral progestational agent, such as Provera or Aygestin. There are distinct changes that take place in the lining of the uterus to eliminate menstrual function.

Testosterone levels- when circulating in adequate serum concentration, will change the thickness and function of the vocal cords for virtually all using it. Occasional individuals will not respond as fully as others, but for most the voice pitch will lower into the male range. The change is complete enough to make the individual's voice masculine, not only in person but on the telephone as well. The F-M individual will not be able to sing in higher ranges as before. This is quite dramatic and quite irreversible.

Hair growth - It takes time, but distinct patterns of hair growth take place. On the face in several years, a full beard is virtually a reality. Chest and extremity hair will be stimulated. The extent varies from one to another, but if hair follicles exist in an area, the hair growth will be evident over time. For a few, male pattern baldness may take place over time as well.

Muscular development - Because of the anabolic or tissue-building property of testosterone, muscle mass will develop and muscle strength will increase. An occasional individual complains of extremity and joint pain, thought to be due to the strain of increased muscle mass on the tendons and their attachments to bone. The individual who exercises and lifts weights will have notable development.

Clitoral change - The clitoris will enlarge and for some the length may be quite notable, up to 6 cm. Again, tissue response is the essential factor, but this is a very striking change for those who experience it.

Skeletal and torso changes - These will not change for the F-M individual. Genetic females are generally smaller, built with a slender, lighter appearance. There will be no skeletal changes in the chest cage or the pelvic region when taking testosterone. The height of the individual remains the same. Estrogen production at puberty closes the epiphysial growth plates located at the ends of long bones. Hands and feet will remain small and facial features will not change in their delicateness. The individual will be a small appearing male.

Potential Problems and Complications for the Female to Male on hormones - F-M

Breast changes - While some distinct cellular changes seen in the microscope in various structures of the breast are evident, the breasts will not become appreciable smaller. With weight reduction, fat storage will diminish and this does affect breast size. The small-breasted individual will be at more advantage than the full-breasted genetic female whose breasts may become somewhat pendulous and dependent. Binding when utilized will be helpful until the breasts are removed and the male chest appearance is created by a surgeon.

Fluid retention - Peripheral edema or fluid retention for some may be a very difficult problem, especially with lower extremity vein incompetency. The natural tendency for sodium and water retention overall is a problem that may require use of diuretics. Some of the weight increase on this therapy is certainly due to this problem.

Weight increase - Even for those who are slim, beginning testosterone can create weight increase difficulties. For those already overweight or obese, this can be a major complication and great care must be taken to become calorie conscious and make every effort to lose weight and then maintain it. A plan for diet sensibility and weight loss with real attention to calorie counting may be a constant way of life. While fluid retention and increased muscle mass can be a part of the problem, eating habits must be reviewed to control this potential. Overweight will contribute to other health problems and this can lead to serious difficulties with hypertension and cardiovascular disease.

Skin changes - The vigorous influence of testosterone on all the glands and structures in the skin accounts for a considerable number of F-M individuals complaining of acne. Intensive facial care may be needed using good cleansing practices and topical acne creams and medications. There may even be a place for antibiotic therapy for a few individuals.

Blood cell changes - Testosterone is a stimulus to making red blood cells in the bone marrow. Some F-M individuals demonstrate very definite changes in their blood hemoglobin and in some of the blood cell measurements that are very typical for a condition called polycythemia. Management of this will depend on the severity of the change brought to this blood building system. Alterations in the testosterone regimen, in addition to the standard treatment for this condition, may be needed.

Liver changes - As in the M-F individual, liver enzyme elevations will be noted in a significant number of hormone users. They will be generally transient elevations coming down to acceptable levels as hormone use continues. Levels that are too high will necessitate interruption of the testosterone regimen and subsequent evaluation. Without significant liver disease, the regimen could be started again but at lower dose and with very gradual increases to appropriate clinical change. If the history and baseline study of liver function indicates that there could be any antecedent liver problem, due very often to alcohol use or prior infection, (i.e. hepatitis) you may not be a candidate for testosterone therapy. Occasional subjects will not have such a prior history and they will have persistently elevated enzymes even after the testosterone is stopped. This must be studied and the potential for certain kinds of liver pathology must be evaluated. A monitoring of liver health is all important throughout the individual's lifetime while using hormones.

Hypertension - Blood pressure elevation can be made worse in already existing hypertension, or a hypertension potential can come to light when testosterone is used. The degree of hypertension and the response to hypertensive therapy will determine whether the testosterone dose is to be continued, to be moderated or stopped altogether. The theoretical concern to be kept in mind, is that testosterone may hasten vessel arteriosclerotic disease and thereby induce heart disease. Hypertension has an effect upon the heart as well. The two in combination can cause very severe health problems. Your physician must be very watchful and very vigorous to treat hypertension, even to the point of stopping hormone therapy. A worsening of preexistent hypertension must be approached with a very appropriate medical plan and that plan must work or the whole regimen must be stopped.

Lipid profile - Masculinizing hormones cause concerning alterations in serum cholesterol, triglycerides and the lipoproteins HDL and LDL. If these substances become extraordinarily elevated or out of proper ratio, they will eventually exert influence upon the blood vessels and their function, creating problems leading to coronary artery disease. In recent reporting of research done by the Free University of Amsterdam, various components of the lipid profile change are somewhat comparable to genetic males not on hormone therapy of any kind. The group of F-M individuals studied on testosterone is small and more individuals and a longer time of observation is necessary, but the inference is clear. F-M individuals on testosterone therapy lose cardio-protective activity with estrogen loss and their risk for significant cardiovascular disease is increased as it is for genetic males who have testosterone production. Once this happens, steps to improve these laboratory determinations and thereby halt that process must be put in place. Diet, exercise, cessation of smoking and appropriate medication when indicated, are very important ingredients in the life of the F-M person. Whether testosterone is to be continued, modified or stopped depends upon patient response to the regimen instituted for an abnormal lipid profile. If improvement does not take place, the hormonal regimen is to be stopped.

Cardiovascular disease - Candidates for testosterone must be selected with no hint of cardiovascular concern in their baseline evaluations. If the cardiovascular system is suspect, proper evaluation is mandatory before any hormone is begun. If cardiovascular disease develops during therapy, the hormonal regimen is halted and the patient evaluated fully with the thought that hormones may or may not be used again. There is one report in the medical literature regarding cardiovascular accident in an F-M individual on testosterone. The loss of cardio-protective value of estrogen along with the fear of premature cardiovascular disease while on testosterone has made some writers speak of this potential in the medical literature. In theory, it is all very possible and more time and more studies are needed. The physician monitoring the F-M individual must be aware of this concern for each and every patient on this hormonal regimen.

Two additional considerations must be kept in mind: The first, emotional changes and the second, phlebitis. By and large, these seem to be lesser concerns than for the M-F on estrogen. Some F-M taking testosterone do report severe emotional alterations. They speak of outbursts of anger and enormous sexual drive and times when energy is outrageous. They are overwhelmed at times by these feelings when first on their hormonal regimen. In time, the greatest part of these exaggerated feelings abate and stability ensues. By and large, they seem to have made very positive adjustments to their lifestyle, and while they have many of the same pressures with family and workplace as do the M-F, their abilities to cope and to adjust seem to be much more positive. Add to this the fact that they are now on the way to effectively accomplishing their goal to make contragender change in using this medication, and they are much happier.

Phlebitis - This is a relatively uncommon complaint for the F-M. It is a serious one nonetheless and it can't be emphasized enough. Your physician must be in constant watchfulness for the development of this disturbing complication.

C - The Surgical Experience
& Early Convalesence - M-F/F-M

"I've been lucky, but a lot of people who have been in my shoes haven't been so fortunate. There are far too many people around today who think that sex change surgery is the answer to all their problems. For most of them, it's merely means trading one set of problems for another. They have no idea of what 'straight' society is like. To them, it's a fantasy land like a child's conception of the grownup world. Many of those who go through sex change surgery think they will be transformed overnight into dazzling creatures who will sweep up a partner and have them at their feet. They think that they will have millionaires clambering to set them up in penthouses. It is quite a come-down for someone like me who had such illusions, to find out that I am just another person and not necessarily a very good-looking one and that I still have to hustle to make a living."

These are the comments of one who had her surgery and then remarks on the reassignment in a crude and hard, though philosophic, way. She wrote a book about her life and all that led up to surgery. Think for a while before going on. This excerpt has relevance to both the M-F as well as F-M.

The information to follow will prepare you for the hospital experience with sex reassignment surgery. It applies to both the M-F as well as F-M individual. While much of this relates to lesser procedures as well, for example, cosmetic surgery, much of the information and orientation is primarily directed to the vaginoplasty in the M-F and the phalloplasty in either single or multiple stages in the F-M individual.

Surgery for both the M-F and F-M individual can be quite an experience. The process can be very lengthy and expensive, both in time and in money. For the M-F, surgery does not mean only loss of male genitalia and creation of a vagina. For some there is much more. There will be breast augmentation for a certain number and facial surgery with creation of a new jawline or a new nose. Alteration of another feature may be a part of the planning. Changes in the appearance of the eyes may be very important. Tracheal shave and with it, voice modulation surgery is commonly sought after. Many other cosmetic changes are available and done with great skill by the most inventive and talented of physicians, the plastic reconstructive surgeon. Revision of scars, changes in the appearance of the ears, the forehead, cheek bones and the chin line, even dental care, may be considered, to mention only a few.

For the F-M, the surgical experience is much more involved and often much more costly. While hormone therapy is considerably more effective for the F-

M than it is for the M-F and certainly much more gratifying; the surgery is much more complicated. There must be removal of the breasts and creation of a male chest. Hysterectomy and removal of the fallopian tubes and ovaries are to be considered as well. This is major surgery and convalescence can be difficult. Finally, the creation of a penis with testes, known as phalloplasty, is a difficult procedure for the patient and the surgeon, and has many drawbacks and often times, many complications.

All of these are important to discuss along with the potential problems associated. Since there is nothing in common with the surgical techniques for the M-F and the F-M, they are presented separately, but some general considerations for both of these individuals are offered. The important general principles in common are noted by the letters that we relied upon before this, (M-F/F-M)

A Discussion About Your Surgeon
- M-F/F-M

If you attend a gender identity center, your referral will be made to a surgeon who works with your other professionals and a search for one is not necessary except in unusual situations. Surgeons who will do cosmetic surgery as well as sex reassignment surgery are available to you through that center. If, however, you live in a city where there are no surgeons caring for the transgendered , you will have the task of finding the right one for you. Unfortunately, they are not many in number, but they do exist in the United States and in Europe and referral can be made to them through your psychologic counselor or your physician if they are knowledgeable as to who will give you good surgical care.

It would be an appropriate approach, to contact a gender center near you for referral to their surgeons. Of course you can always make a request to support groups and Informational Resource groups such as the **International Foundation for Gender Education** (IFGE), Waltham, Massachusetts for the surgeons who are involved with plastic, reconstruction and sex reassignment surgical procedures, anywhere in the world.

Lastly, you could make a direct request to the Harry Benjamin Association for surgeon referral anywhere throughout the world.

For those who are looking to have the services of a plastic surgeon for breast augmentation or facial cosmetic surgery, generally any or all plastic surgeons are trained to do these procedures quite expertly. The problem is not in their skill but finding one in your community who is empathetic and who will care for you as a transgendered person, particularly if you have not as yet had reassignment surgery. They are reluctant and you will have to do the familiar "finger-walking through the Yellow Pages" exercise. You will have to interview and evaluate them. To travel great distances to those who do care for the transgendered doing plastic procedures seems to me to be unnecessary, but it may, in fact, become necessary should you not find a plastic surgeon in your region who is responsive and responsible.

For the F-M individual, the search will be moderately harder, for your preliminary procedures before phalloplasty are involved with tissue removal, not revision. Removal of so-called normal tissue (breasts, uterus, ovaries) that is not associated with disease or pathology is not generally approved of by hospital review committees and third party payers. Your surgeon does not ordinarily do these procedures unless pathology or disease does exist. If his/her practice in transsexual care is known to his/her hospital administration, then generally he/she will have no problem with his/her care of you. He/She must inform the administration of his/her hospital and certain medical staff committees of his/her expertise in these techniques and the fact that he/she will have periodic hospital admission of patients who are having this kind of surgical procedure. The problem then may be with third party payers. The cost for these procedures in the absence of pathology may not be paid for by an insurance company. They view this kind of surgery generally as cosmetic or experimental and your request for their payment of your expenses will be refused except in special instances. These things have to be discussed with your operating surgeon beforehand, especially if this is to be paid for out of pocket. You want to know what his/her fees are and what the cost for hospitalization and anesthesia care are so that you are fully informed and have adequate funding.

Sex reassignment surgery is complicated, and lengthy. It requires one who does this procedure often and who has perfected the technique, and understands the problems and their solutions. There are not a great many surgeons who are so skilled. You will make your selection based on the sources for referral that we have mentioned before this. You may need to interview several in order to find the one you can work with and feel confident in. As we mentioned before this, surgeons who are skilled in sex reassignment surgery are known to the Harry Benjamin Association and to IFGE and they do this kind of surgery in volume. Hence, they generally have great experience. When circumstances are such that you cannot find a skilled or responsive surgeon in the area in which you live, travel and increased expense in many instances may be the case. It may, however, be your only option.

What to Look for in Your Surgeon - M-F/F-M

There are certain things that you will want to find in your surgeon. His/Her credentials and degrees are hanging on his/her wall and they tell you something of how well he/she is trained and whether or not he/she is board certified. Board certification in various specialties means that the physician has passed rigid evaluation and examination procedures conducted by specialists and teachers in that area of care. But that is not enough. There is more for you to look for in your mutual evaluations of each other.

To begin with, in all your visits with your health care professional, but especially in your initial visit, you must present yourself quite appropriately. Your appearance must be tasteful and that first impression made with how you look, how you conduct yourself and how you speak is so important. You want to be knowledgeable and capable of discussing the procedures planned. It's true, you are not medically trained, but your prior knowledge and your intelligence should put you in an excellent position to know what it is that is planned and what it is that you can expect.

Your doctor on the other hand should be empathetic, pleasant and willing to discuss the procedures planned. He/She should give insight into what results will be expected, and what complications could take place and what the solutions for those complications are. He/She should be very willing to discuss and, to give information to you about all that you will experience. You want to be satisfied about what he/she will do in the operating room. You want to know if he/she agrees with your concepts of the surgery. You want very thorough discussion of the immediate hospital convalescence and you want good insight into what things to expect in the late convalescence when you have returned to your home.

Important Areas of Discussion Between You and your Surgeon - M-F/F-M

By and large, there are some generalities that should certainly come into a discussion between you and your operating physician. They are these:

a. Did your surgeon receive appropriate documentation from your mental health-care professional and from the physician involved with your general medical health care and hormonal therapy? Your psychologic counselor and/or psychiatrist should supply a thorough insight into you, the person, and give in a brief, concise, but accurate way, the evaluation and preparative process that you worked through together. The recommendation for surgery letter is not really enough.

The surgeon must have accurate insight into your general health, any special problems or medical conditions that existed before or since hormones were started, and a list of recent laboratory data, all to give assurance that you are a proper candidate for the surgery planned. There must be opportunity to communicate with the medical physician, if the need is there, to clarify or emphasize some point of information. The surgeon may want to repeat some studies to be certain that all is in good order.

b. It will be important to discuss with your surgeon the medications you use, prior to surgery. **Hormones should be interrupted four to six weeks before the procedure is to be done**. This is an important consideration substantiated by reports in the medical literature. Postoperative phlebitis is a concern at all times, no matter what the surgery. It is more particularly so when individuals are using estrogen and similar considerations would be in mind for those using testosterone or anti-androgens as well. There is also the real danger of blood clot (embolism) to the lungs, and this is most serious. It should be discussed.

Other medications need to be reviewed and alterations or additions in dosage may be necessary. This information should be shared with the anesthesiologist by you directly. Individuals with diabetes, hypertension or cardiac problems, all have unique concerns the surgeon and anesthesiologist must discuss in their care of you in surgery and in the first few postoperative days. Please bring these matters into your preoperative discussion.

Ask also how you can prepare yourself for the surgical procedure. Should you prepare your body with shaving the operative site or washing with antibacterial soaps for a week or two before the surgery? Will you be given prophylactic antibiotics to reduce the possibilities of a postoperative infection in the wound or in the bladder? Just what are the possibilities of these developing in this doctor's experience? **YOU SHOULD ASK!**

c. There should be discussion between you and the operating surgeon about test results sent to him and additional testing he plans to order for you. Because it is a very important consideration, you should discuss the potential for a blood transfusion, if needed. What are his criteria? What safeguards exist in the hospital for testing donor blood? If you are to be operated on in your own city or near to it, you could put your own blood "in storage" with the local blood bank and it would be kept there and reserved for you should the need arise. This technique is not generally possible if you are traveling a distance for your procedure. The matter of possible transfusion certainly should be in your discussion. There is always the possibility of serious blood loss no matter what the procedure, and no matter what the precautions taken. Hopefully, the loss of blood will not be great enough to require transfusion. Blood transfusions nowadays carry risk, though not as great as in days past, but there is possibility of contamination with hepatitis and AIDS viruses. Blood banks employ very careful protocols for collection and testing of donor blood and transfusion reactions and contamination are quite rare but still great precaution is a must.

d. There should be discussion and planning for physicians to care for you once you are discharged from the hospital and sent home. This is most important and you must arrange for that medical care to be in place **before** you leave home for your surgery. A medical doctor for purely medical concerns should be arranged for before the surgery, particularly if these concerns exist before the procedure or should they develop during the hospitalization. This person I refer to as your **Home Medical Doctor or Physician.**

An 'at home' surgeon who will care for post-surgical problems that arise in the hospital convalescence and need follow up once you have returned home, must be arranged for **before** surgery. That surgeon is necessary also for follow-up routine evaluations once you are at home. There is the possibility that you can discuss some of this with the doctor who manages your major health care. He or she can make referral to a responsive surgeon in your area. You may want to have a consultation with that surgeon prior to leaving for your surgery, such that you will make smooth the pathway for after surgical care and treatment, when necessary. I refer to that physician as your "at home surgical doctor."

Your operating surgeon must know who those doctors are and must, in my view, send to them a discharge summary (a review of your surgery and postoperative convalescence). A copy of your operative report, pertinent laboratory data, and instructions relative to special circumstances or problems must also be sent. A line of communication should be established between your surgeon and your physicians at home, for there will be a need for information exchange. Your surgeon should not "disappear" or absent himself from your care because you are hundreds or thousands of miles away. Any problems developing when at home convalescing that may not be within the expertise of your home physician should permit ready access to your operating doctor. This is the way it would be if you were operated in your hometown. Distance should make no difference and you must prepare for this. Appropriate exchange of medical information and availability for consultation is not to be missing in your care.

If you are to be operated some distance from home and cannot make appropriate post-surgical visits to the **operating** surgeon but must schedule them with an 'at home' surgeon, you should try if possible to stay for a time in the area where your operating surgeon practices. This can be a costly matter, I know, but extra time near that doctor is valuable since some immediate problems can be dealt with much more completely by the operating physician. Inquiry about facilities and conveniences near his or her office or the hospital is quite important. Perhaps a friend or even a care person that your doctor uses for such situations will be available to you. It certainly does take planning, doesn't it? It's all very worth the while. This is a major step and a costly one and has such an important impact on your future life. Why not be thorough and sure of it all. Take the right steps. These are all points for detailed discussion with your operating surgeon. This opportunity must be allowed to you. When the surgeon does allow this, and you have adequate information about the procedure, the convalescence in the hospital and at home, then you will feel quite assured and confident.

The Hospital Admission - M-F/F-M

In most instances, hospitalization will begin with an admission the day before the planned procedure. In some hospitals, and for some procedures however, admission is planned for early in the morning on the day of the surgery, and if what you are having done is an outpatient procedure, then you will be admitted through the admissions office that same day. Your doctor will give you insight into what the standard approach is. The remarks to follow have to do with admission one day prior to the surgical procedure.

For whatever that procedure may be, in most instances, you should have someone with you on entry and at discharge. Going into the hospital, you will be flustered and anxious. That kind companion can remember what you might forget and help you forget what you shouldn't remember. Leaving the hospital, you will be weak and truly you will feel assaulted and damaged. A strong arm and a happy heart next to you will be a wonderful benefit to you.

You will go to the admissions office on entry to the hospital, where plans for payment come to completion and where your room will be assigned. From there you may be taken to the laboratory for final testing, although those tests may have been done several days before as an outpatient. Some studies may be a repeat of what you have had in the past, for instance, x-rays and electrocardiogram testing. There will be routine blood and urine studies, blood cell counts, measurements of electrolytes and kidney function, perhaps liver enzymes, blood sugar and there will be tests for AIDS and hepatitis antibodies as part of the preoperative work up. Your blood will be typed and matched and some blood coagulation studies may be done as well. With these things completed, you will be sent to your hospital floor and once in your room, you will meet your nurse or nurse's aides. There you will be asked to change to hospital garb, though you may be allowed to wear your own for variable periods of time. If you did not go to the laboratory from admissions, one or several lab technicians may come to see you at this point.

Your nurse will explain to you your preparation for the surgery planned and give you insight into what is involved in getting you ready for the operation. After an evening meal (your last for a time, for you will be permitted nothing to eat or drink after midnight) and final preparations, such as shaving various body areas, washing those areas and perhaps enemas, when needed, you most probably will be given prophylactic antibiotics to reduce postoperative infection. Any drug allergies that you may have encountered in the past should have been discussed at some time before this. You may have a visit from the anesthesiologist and your surgeon sometime before you close your eyes. Their discussions should clarify any concerns in their minds and in yours. They should give you assurance and confidence in their talk with you.

Finally, you will be offered sleep medication. Take it, it will be a great help, for you need a good night's sleep. It's very important.

The Morning of Surgery is Here - M-F/F-M

The night duty nurse will waken you, though you may have apprehension enough to greet her when she comes into the room. You will be asked to bathe briefly and to use the bathroom facilities. Then a preoperative medication may be given to you by your nurse. This helps to relax you and contains other medicines to make the anesthesia induction progress smoothly.

You will put on a special surgical gown. There will be no breakfast tray and you must not drink **anything** nor take any medication on your own. An orderly or another nurse will bring a litter into your room for transport.

You will be transported to the operating suite and you will be held for a short time in a preparation room before going into the operating room. Sometimes it is in this area, although sometimes in the operating room itself, that you will be interviewed once again by a member of the anesthesia staff and it will be at that time that an intravenous needle and line delivering fluids to your veins will be started. It is through that line that a sleep-inducing medication will be given to you, and then your awareness and conscious involvement in what takes place thereafter is gone. You are now progressing on the pathway that you have wanted to travel for so long.

Male to Female
Reassignment Surgery - M-F

Ancillary Procedures

For the M-F individual, surgical reassignment will not be as difficult or as prolonged as it will be for the F-M person. Overall expense will be considerably less as well, and while a good deal more perfection has been accomplished by surgeons over the world in accomplishing all the goals of the M-F person, these doctors are not complacent and still seek to add refinements to their techniques and to lessen complication rates.

Ancillary procedures will possibly be a part of the overall reassignment and these include breast augmentation, face and skull cosmetic techniques, tracheal reduction, voice pitch modulation and liposuction procedures. Before looking at genitalia reassignment, we should evaluate these ancillary approaches.

Breast surgery - Adequate hormonal therapy will probably accomplish all that is to be expected in breast growth after about two years of continuous use. If the regimen has been an optimal one, individual tissue response will be maximal in this time period. If one is comfortable with the degree of development, then nothing more need be considered. Many are not and in wanting more breast prominence, there needs to be a realistic approach always in mind. Breast size should be in keeping with what is proportional to one's height and chest girth. If more is desired, then surgery can surely be done to augment. The technique of augmentation should be discussed completely with your surgeon and that physician should have much experience with all forms of surgery to augment the breast and to diminish it. Free substances (that is, non-encapsulated) should not be used to create more breast size. The most important prohibition is that free silicone is never to be used. **NEVER!**

Formerly, breast implants wherein silicone was placed were utilized tremendously by plastic surgeons. At this time however, a great deal of controversy exists as to whether this is a safe and appropriate technique in order to accomplish this goal. I will not comment for or against the use of silicone breast implants. Suffice it to say that most surgeons will not place them at this time. The controversy has not been settled and the medical/legal issues associated could be quite concerning. They will, however, place saline filled prostheses (salt solution) and they do this in several different ways. In brief, the techniques now utilized are these:

1. Insertion **beneath** natural breast tissue but **above** the chest muscle layer. This is accomplished through several different incision sites.

   The insertion above the chest muscle layer - Entry to a space created beneath breast tissue and above the muscle layer is often through an incision in the areola (or nipple) area of the breast. The incision follows the margin of the lower half of this pigmented area around the nipple. It is generally a small incision and can heal with only a fine line, hardly noticeable, if the surgeon uses good cosmetic technique to close the incision, and no infection takes place.

   Other incision sites are below the breast crease which is really quite hidden by the enlarged breasts, or in the axilla (arm pit). This incision is also an attempt to hide the entry site. The saline filled prostheses are placed symmetrically and at the right height beneath breast tissue and should stay where they are placed. The body's reaction in time is to encapsulate the foreign body, the substance-filled prostheses, but occasionally the insert may slip on one side and the appearance may be an asymmetric placement. The body's natural tendency to encapsulate can sometimes act as a problem for individuals and encapsulation sometimes leads to unusual dimpling, scarring, or discomfort.

2. Insertion beneath **both** natural breast tissue and the chest muscle layer. This also is approached through several incision sites.

The insertion beneath the chest muscle layer - The optimal incision for this technique is entry just below the breast crease. Access to the muscle and creation of a space beneath it and the skeletal wall is easier this way. The axillary incision can be utilized, though the muscle is stouter and more resistant to being lifted in this approach. The circum- areolar incision cannot be used at all for entry in this technique. It is too small and right on the breast tissue. Access to the muscle to place the pros- thesis under it is terribly difficult by this route. The value of beneath the muscle placement of the saline filled envelope is that once it is in place, it will not be displaced - slippage is quite minimized. Some surgeons feel that a more natural appearance is achieved as well.

Skull and face cosmetic procedures - There are a great many cosmetic approaches to feminize the face and head of the M-F transsexual. Plastic and reconstructive surgeons have such skill and imaginative approach to changing the masculine appearance into the feminine. They can alter the eyelids in order to create much more openness to the eyes and to lend a youthful look. Erasing skin lines around the mouth and eyes with dermabrasion and peels also give youth and femininity to the older face. Changes in nose shape, in chin, and jawline are very helpful in feminizing. Lifting tissue to soften and smooth the cheeks, neck and forehead and removing under the skin fat collections (liposuction) are other techniques. Insertion of prostheses to elevate the cheek tissue and even change the skull above the eyes (the forehead) to look more like the female forehead is very possible and positive, bringing a feminine look to the individual.

You need to discuss in detail what would be appropriate for you. A very promi- nent chin or a heavy jaw when altered will improve your appearance notably. But is it for you? Can you afford this "icing on the cake"? That has to be discussed as well, for with very, very few exceptions, this is money out of pocket. It is all cosmetic surgery and next to none of these procedures will be paid for by third party payers. Some doctors feel it essential and insist on these cosmetic procedures to accompany the genital reassignment procedure. I don't see how this insistence can be justified. Some individuals can barely pay for the genital reassignment surgery out of pocket. Some individuals don't feel these cosmetic niceties are necessary in their own perception of self. For those in whom "passability" will be improved greatly, these techniques can be discussed, but they must not be mandatory for consideration of transition and eventual reassignment surgery.

Tracheal shave and voice pitch surgery - These are techniques not essential for the candidate for reassignment, but are certainly very helpful. A very prominent "Adam's apple" can be reduced measurably, and surgeons that do voice modulation surgery will often combine the tracheal shave with a voice pitch technique they have experience in performing. Some surgeons do only the shave procedure. If you are looking for both changes, select a surgeon who can do both at the same time. They are done under local anesthesia and the incision can be very nicely hidden with careful placement and good healing.

The results with the tracheal shave are complete and satisfying to most having the procedure. The voice modulation techniques are not always so successful. You must discuss with your voice modulation surgeon, his/her technique and his/her experience, and it is reasonable to make inquiry as to what his/her success rate has been **in doing this procedure**. Not many surgeons do this operation and the number of patients who have prolonged success, achieving a voice with a female range, pitch and quality that is acceptable, can be quite variable.

It would seem that those who have voice therapy with an experienced voice pathologist or therapist before surgery, and for a time after it, can be assured of greater success. This is a relatively gray area and you should make very indepth inquiry of those surgeons that are known to do this kind of work.

Liposuction techniques - Unwanted fat can be removed from various places on the body. Most commonly, fat is taken from the abdomen, but the thighs and buttocks are also sites to be remolded. While it can be very helpful and very flattering, you should view it as truly a surgical approach. It does hurt afterwards and there can be considerable blood loss. Fat embolism, and very infrequently fatalities, have been reported in the medical literature. The suction site can be quite bruised for some time and infections can also be a part of the convalescence.

Tummy tucks - This is a procedure wherein excess and sagging skin can be removed from the abdominal wall. Recovery can be very difficult and prolonged. Infection in the wound is a very real possibility and scarring can be very significant. Weight loss programs along with muscle toning exercises should be utilized fully before embarking on a procedure of this sort. In selecting a surgeon to perform this kind of surgery, one must be quite assured of his/her skill and his/her prior experience.

Tatoo removal - Variable amounts of success can be expected with removal of tattoos. It depends upon the size and location of the tatoo primarily. Direct surgical excision may be applicable in many instances, but with the development of laser techniques, this has been a very efficient alternate in many instances. This must be considered on an individual basis and discussion with one or several plastic surgeons may be important to evaluate all potential approaches for the tatoo area(s).

The Goals to be Accomplished in
Genital Reassignment Surgery - M-F

The ideal results to accomplish with genital reassignment surgery in the M-F individual are as follows:

1. The appearance of the external genitalia should be very authentic. The labia majora (the external vaginal lips) should be correct in size and in length and join in the midline appropriately above the clitoris. The labia minora should be small and correctly positioned. The vaginal opening should not be gaping or too open and the neovaginal lining should not protrude or prolapse to a point beyond the labia minora.

2. The vaginal length and width should be appropriate. To be able to place two fingers (the index and middle fingers) as does the gynecologist when conducting a pelvic exam is an appropriate width. A six inch depth is quite adequate as well. There should be no shelf, nor directional deviation, and no closure or stenosis at any point in the neovaginal length. The vaginal angle must be correct for comfortable sexual relations. The vaginal opening should not become narrow or be restricted (stenosis) in the late convalescence period.

3. The vestibule should be sensate. This means that the neovaginal opening should have sensitivity when touched and lead to erotic feelings and response. This is the same sensation that should result when the neoclitoris is touched by the partner's tongue, fingers or penis.

4. As time goes on with healing, there should be less and less difficulty with neovaginal drainage or discharge, and there should be no bleeding or spotting either spontaneously or after a sexual experience.

5. In the long term, there should be no loss of vaginal depth, no vaginal protrusion or prolapse, and no vaginal stenosis at the opening or at any point in the entire length of the vagina. Very importantly, urinary function should be uncomplicated. The urethral opening must be in the proper relationship to structures around it, which means that it should have been placed appropriately at the time of primary surgery. There should be proper direction of the urinary stream and no evidence of urethral narrowing or closure (stenosis) which will cause urine to spray or be misdirected. Urinary infections should not be frequent for any postoperative person. While these infections can develop spontaneously on uncommon occasions, or can take place after sexual relations, this should be an uncommon occurrence.

Genital Reassignment Procedures - M-F

1. *Skin grafts* - These grafts are portions of skin taken from several different sites. The important thing for you to be aware of is that full thickness grafts in contrast to split thickness grafts have much more chance for viability. These grafts are used to line the tunnel developed to be the vagina. The potential for their survival and their adherence to the recipient tissue in the tunnel, made to be the neovagina, is much more assured. Full thickness grafts may be taken from the groin area or the thigh and are moved into place with blood supply intact. In other words, they are spoken of as being pedicled. This helps strongly to insure viability. Dilation postoperatively is usually not needed and the neovagina does not close or undergo stenosis. Some surgeons endorse this technique very heartily. There is one note of concern that you should be aware of however. There have been reports in the medical literature of cancer developing in the skin grafts used to construct the neovagina. There are currently seven reported cases in various medical journals. This, however, is not a common problem, yet it does emphasize the fact that you should have a yearly gynecologic exam with vaginal wall pap smears done if your neovagina is to be fashioned from any kind of skin graft, either full thickness or split.

2. *Penile skin (inversion technique)* - In a variety of techniques the penile **skin** is dissected from the penis and the penile **tissue** is discarded. The urethra which formerly traversed the length of the penis is shortened and placed appropriately above the vaginal tunnel which is lined by the penile skin. In some techniques, the glans of the penis is preserved and when the penile skin is inverted, the glans looks like a female cervix (this is the mouth of the uterus which extends down into the vagina). In some techniques, it is not saved. A portion of it can be saved, as we will discuss later, and will be used to form the neoclitoris. If the individual is circumcised, this skin loss could subtract from the neovaginal length and a skin graft may be needed to lengthen the newly formed vagina. In some techniques, the scrotal skin will be joined to penile skin to form the back or posterior wall of the vagina. Many surgeons would rather that no circumcision was done when the individual was quite young because the foreskin adds to the vaginal length they want so much to obtain for their patient. Many are troubled also by penile shortening or shrinkage as it occurs for a considerable number who are taking hormones. This also will necessitate the need for skin grafting to insure adequate vaginal length. The inversion technique is one of the most popular procedures utilized currently. Ideally, it is much better if skin grafts are not associated with this particular technique.

3. *Scrotal skin* - Some surgeons will use the scrotal skin to form the new vagina discarding the penis entirely. The need to use skin flaps or skin grafts is frequently the case in this procedure. While this technique is technically possible it is not as adequate as the penile inversion approach.

4. *Scrotal skin with penile skin*- The scrotum once the testes are removed, can be utilized either to form the labia or to help in the construction of the vagina. The scrotal skin can be combined with penile skin to form a tube.

The penile skin is the top or anterior wall and the scrotal skin the back or posterior wall of this tube. The tube is then placed in the tunnel thereby lining it. Regardless of what your surgeon will determine to do, it will be important for you to raise the question of hair growth inside the vagina when scrotal skin is part of the newly constructed organ. You should ask your surgeon how to eliminate or greatly diminish hair growth before surgery takes place. This can be a difficult problem for some. It is discomforting with sexual intercourse and at other times, there are matted hairballs that form in the top of the vagina and combined with vaginal secretions will be passed periodically.

5. *Colovaginoplasty (rectosigmoid vaginoplasty)* - This technique requires no donor sites from various areas of the body. Instead, it utilizes a segment of large bowel. It is utilized as a primary procedure by some surgeons, though most believe it should be offered primarily only if the penis is too short and skin flaps are not feasible. Most surgeons, however, will not use this as an initial or primary procedure, but rather prefer to use it as a secondary procedure when a prior operation has met with failure or its complications are not repairable.

One of the concerns with this procedure is the need to enter the abdominal cavity and to perform a large bowel resection. In skilled experienced hands, the risks with this procedure are lessened considerably, but it does complicate the operation. In the techniques mentioned before this, there is no planned entry into the abdomen.

Essentially, a segment of rectosigmoid (large bowel) is separated and isolated from the bowel retaining its blood supply, and the divided bowel segments are reunited. The separated bowel segment is swung down into the tunnel created for it, after removal of the penis and testes, and the preservation and placement of a portion of the urethra. In essence, the inner surface of the large bowel segment is the neovaginal lining. In recent surgical experience with this technique, small skin grafts are used at the new vaginal opening and scrotal and penile skin is used to construct the labia. Small skin grafts tend to reduce, if not eliminate, blood spotting and discharge from the new vagina. Two surgical teams operate at the same time to perform this procedure. Champions of this technique point out that virtually unlimited vaginal length is obtainable, that lubrication is natural and adequate and that no dilatation is necessary postoperatively. They report also that erotic sensitivity is accomplished quite successfully.

Those surgeons who would use this operation as a secondary procedure, or consider it hesitantly at any time, point out that vaginal discharge can be a very troublesome problem and that vaginal bleeding, particularly after sexual experience, can be a very disturbing difficulty, even with the skin flaps placed at the opening of the vagina.

The fact that a bowel resection is a part of the procedure does raise concern. The potential for serious abdominal infection does pose question. However, in experienced hands, the technique does have to be considered seriously when a primary procedure fails or is unsatisfactory.

The Construction of the Neoclitoris

Several techniques are utilized to create a clitoris. All efforts should be made to accomplish several things in the clitoral construction.

a)   An aesthetic appearance
b)   A sensate organ
c)   No loss to this organ in appearance through retraction or change in size or in sensation with late loss of nerve supply

Techniques currently in use:

The use of penile erectile tissue - The tissue in the penis that becomes enlarged due to inflow of blood with sexual excitement producing erection is twofold, the corpus spongiosum and the corpus cavernosum. In all surgical procedures, the corpus cavernosum should be removed completely in the surgical technique, along with the greatest portion of spongiosum. However, a small amount of spongiosum is retained attached to the urethra and along with a segment of urethra is positioned appropriately above the neovaginal opening with the blood and nerve supply preserved. It should be placed appropriately, and some surgeons feel that this combination of tissue creates a very sensate organ. Some patients do not agree and in time, experience a loss of the neoclitoris anatomically through tissue shrinkage. Some patients with sexual excitement may have too much blood entrapment in residual spongiosum to the point of creating a great deal of pain and partial obstruction to the vaginal canal and then experience need to interrupt the sexual experience. This is not an ideal result. You should discuss this possibility with your surgeon and inquire as to what solutions are possible should these discomforts arise.

The use of the Glans Penis - The end of the penis, or the "knob end" or head of the organ is called the glans penis. This is quite sensitive and with sexual excitement, because of its nerve supply, transmits a very erotic message to the brain. The most sensitive place on the glans is the ridge, known as the corona. When a surgeon develops a wedge of glans tissue preserving the corona to use as the neoclitoris, he/she can construct a very sensate structure. He/she has the choice of preserving the blood and nerve supply (neurovascular bundle) in a very careful dissection, or he or she can cut the blood and nerve supply using the wedge as a free graft. When placing it appropriately above the neovagina, they will use microsurgical technique to reconnect the blood vessels and nerves, thereby restoring to the wedge, adequate vascularization and sensation.

Overall this technique seems to be somewhat superior to the urethral spongiosum neoclitoris and the dissection of the wedge with the neurovascular bundle intact, seems to be better as well. There is the danger of tissue death or slough when the neurovascular bundle is severed, shortened, and reconnected. It is worth talking about this aspect of the technique with your surgeon.

The construction of the labia

These very important parts of the new anatomy are constructed differently and at different times by various surgeons. Some will create the outer labia or labia majora at the same time they create the neovagina. Others will delay labial construction to an appropriate time after vaginoplasty, usually six months or more. The labial construction can be done with scrotal skin if the scrotum was not used in the newly created vagina, and that could be done in the primary procedure. If scrotal skin is part of the neovagina, then skin flaps must be used and they are taken from the inguinal and inner thigh areas.

Both approaches and the various techniques utilized are reasonable and successful, the only drawback being a secondary procedure for labia construction that some surgeons prefer in genital reassignment. This should be discussed as well. The secondary procedure need not be done by the same surgeon; hence, travel and expense may not be quite as difficult. Some reassigned individuals never have labial construction and this depends on how anatomically accurate they choose to be. In any event, construction of the labia majora and minora, whether from scrotal skin, perineal tissue or from grafts, can contribute notably to the authenticity and aesthetics of the newly created genital region. Success with this surgical reconstruction is generally very complete.

Is there a place for castration alone when certain criteria are met?

In my opinion, the answer to this question is yes. There are three categories wherein individuals can be placed, and when meeting the appropriate criteria, castration alone without removal of the penis or creation of a vagina could be considered.

1. There are individuals who take a very appropriate hormonal regimen to feminize, have experienced electrolysis, and live as women on a full-time basis. These women do not intend to have Sex Reassignment Surgery and consequently self-label themselves as transgenderists or non-operative Transsexuals. They may in fact undergo surgical procedures, cosmetic in nature, either facial techniques, augmentation mammoplasty and other kinds of physical alteration in order to augment their feminine appearance, yet they will not alter their genitalia. Orchiectomy would be an option for this group since it allows them to lower hormonal dosage, thereby lessening the risk of complication. In addition, it adds greatly to the feminization process. Prophylaxis against development of cardiovascular disease and prostatic disease, either benign or malignant, is a very real possibility for this group as well.

2. Another group to be considered, and possibly one more difficult to identify, may be allowed to choose orchiectomy while planning definitive reassignment surgery at a much later date. The reasons for the delay could be numerous and must be explored with their therapists. The orchiectomy could be a more effective aid to feminization during the transition time (real life test) and lessen the stresses and concerns that the preoperative transsexual may have in being able to socialize.

3. A third group to be considered, consists of those whose age would be beyond allowance for surgery or who might have health concerns that would eliminate them as candidates for a complete sex reassignment procedure. Because the orchiectomy can be done under local anesthesia in many instances, risks for these individuals could be minimized considerably and they could accomplish the feminization that they so earnestly seek, even with age or health-related prohibitions.

Presently, physicians are very hesitant to allow this procedure. They fear that individuals may have second thoughts after such an irreversible surgical approach. Actually, individuals might not have the thorough psychologic evaluation insisted upon by surgeons and sponsored by the Harry Benjamin Gender Dysphoria Association in many instances, and this could lead to repercussion. While injectable masculinization hormones would help greatly to replace lost testicular function, that is not the ideal, of course. Yet, with criteria formulated by the Harry Benjamin Association and rigidly adhered to by member surgeons --- this is an approachable problem. Few surgeons or urologists countrywide will consider this approach at this time. There is need for consideration and discussion about this and hopefully with appropriate Harry Benjamin Association evaluation and sanction, there will be in time allowance for this procedure on a limited and selected basis.

Female to Male Reassignment Surgery - F-M

Some preliminary thoughts regarding surgery for the F-M individual

Just when various surgical approaches will be discussed with your doctor and then implemented will likely depend upon a number of factors. Probably there will be no venture into this area of discussion until the F-M individual is well into transition, or the "real life test". It may be that some professionals may require a notable period of time of hormone use before beginning a discussion of the various surgical techniques.

It will be important for full-breasted F-M individuals to consider mastectomy soon after entering the real life test period. Binding the breasts can be insufficient to make easy this period of time, especially when facial hair growth begins and voice changes are evident. Binding is also uncomfortable and a nuisance. The breasts are a very prominent part of the female anatomy. Early planning for eliminating this obvious insignia of femaleness in important. On the other hand, menses are a private event, easily hidden and very likely soon eliminated with hormonal use. Hence for many, there may be no urgency in having a hysterectomy associated with removal of the tubes and ovaries. Recent development in techniques allow for removal of the uterus at the time of phalloplasty. It should be planned for, in my estimate, whether it is done in association with the phalloplasty technique or independent of this. While it is most probable that no potential for problem or serious disease is a threat if the uterus is left in place, psychologically it is appropriate to have it removed.

There are reports in the medical literature, however, that a fair proportion of F-M individuals have what is known as polycystic ovarian disease, and if this exists, this condition could pose some measure of difficulty in obtaining appropriate testosterone effect, or could even cause lower abdominal discomforts should these cysts become symptomatic. It just doesn't make sense to retain the tubes and ovaries when an individual has made a definite decision to assume the contragender.

Phalloplasty is a very difficult procedure and a number of techniques have been devised to accomplish all that is needed and important to the F-M individual. In doing this procedure, esthetics and functionality are always to be kept in mind. An organ as close to normal appearing as possible is an important goal. This is the ideal. The ability to stand to urinate and to urinate comfortably without problem is realizable. Good sexual function hopefully can be accomplished and this should include comfortable and satisfactory penetration with methods to produce erections and satisfying performance for the F-M person and his partner. The phallus should be sensate or have sensitivity to touch and erogenous stimulus. This also is the ideal. In many ways in the past, the surgery has been very inadequate and disappointing, but currently, some of the problems of the past are being solved. The discussion of the techniques and ways to accomplish a successful phalloplasty will be helpful to you and prepare you for appropriate conversation with your surgeon.

Breast surgery

One of the goals of reduction mammoplasty must be removal of all, or as much as is possible, of the breast tissue on both sides. This is important not only for the cosmetic results which is foremost in the mind of both the F-M individual and the surgeon, but there is also another consideration. Academic as it may be, with breast tissue left behind, there might be the potential of breast cancer development. While it is true that the F-M individual will be using testosterone which will counter estrogenic effects on the breasts and eventually it can be assumed that all ovarian tissue will be removed, thereby removing the most active source of estrogen, still there could be the possibility of malignant disease developing here with cessation of testosterone for whatever reason at a later time. Specific health reasons complicating the overall plan to transfer to a contragender state may be the reason for stopping hormones. Hence, all tissue on the chest wall and that breast tissue which may extend into the arm pit, called the axillary region, should be taken out as completely as is possible. A F-M individual who is not immediately pursuing surgery, and in fact may even delay it for some time, will likely not be having mammography in the years to come, nor will he be doing self-breast examinations. Hence, surgical thoroughness is necessary.

In addition, there are cosmetic effects to keep in mind. To begin with, the inframammary crease must be eliminated. Another factor that must be kept in mind is the manner in which the areola area and the nipple are managed. The areola should be reduced when it is necessary, and the nipple can be retained as a free flap or kept attached at one place to the chest wall in order to retain the blood and nerve supply, thereby helping to retain some of the sensitivity and viability. A plastic surgeon must understand the technique for making the nipple areola area complex smaller. Proper nipple placement is essential on the chest wall. Problems with healing are to be avoided as best possible or solved efficiently should they arise. It should be kept in mind, however, that sometimes the nipple does lose its sensitivity and it may not be the focal point in sexual arousal that it was some time before.

Scarring should be minimized. Unsightly incisions should be avoided even though chest hair growth is anticipated. Techniques will vary based on whether the person is small or large breasted, but sculpturing of the chest must be done with care and skill to create the male appearance. There must be no pockets or abnormal places over the chest wall. The appropriate thickness of breast eminences as they appear in the genetic male chest is the goal. With small breasts, a small incision can be made on the areola and the glandular and ductal tissue of the breast can be removed quite sufficiently through this small entry. When dealing with large and dependent breasts, larger incisions will be needed to take out all of the tissue and reduce excess skin. The potential for infection, unsightly scarring and possible keloid formation in the scars is all too real and should be avoided as is best possible.

Binding of the breasts as it is practiced before surgery is a potential for real problem. The skin can be damaged with tight binding and scars may result. In addition, the very tight binding causes the breast to be very dependent resulting in deep elongation and flattening of the breasts in some individuals. This creates excessive skin that must be removed to shape the chest and reposition the nipples properly. The problem of creating a male chest with a minimum of scarring is complicated by this preoperative maneuver to de-emphasize the breasts.

Only surgeons who have experience with these techniques should be consulted. Liposuction and ultrasound, called liposculpturing, are used a great deal. Your physician should give very clear instruction to you as to what will be done. He should give insight into what is to be expected and should dispel any fantasies or misconceptions regarding the results. On occasion, psychologic counseling is needed before and after this kind of surgery.

Hysterectomy

Removal of the uterus can be done in several ways and there may be definite reasons why a surgeon may select a particular technique for removal. If the uterus is enlarged with fibroid tumors, a benign enlargement, an abdominal approach may be indicated. If the ovaries have pathology that need special attention, the abdominal incision may be once again selected. Vaginal hysterectomy is possible and in skilled hands, the tubes and ovaries can be removed by this route. Laparoscopy is another feasible approach for removal of all the internal genitalia, but it takes a great deal more operating time than an abdominal or vaginal approach. It may be that a F-M individual wants an hysterectomy done prior to his planning for the creation of a phallus and a male perineum. This can be done without sex reassignment surgery, which may be delayed to a later time, but the vagina should be kept patent and accessible, for some reassignment surgeons will use vaginal wall tissue to create an urethral extension from the native urethra to the new phallus. Vaginal obliteration can then be a part of the phallic construction phase. Should it be that removal of the uterus, tubes and ovaries has not been done prior to a reassignment procedure, these organs can be removed when the phalloplasty is performed, or they can be removed when the urethral extension is to be done prior to phalloplasty if a staged approach to reassignment is planned on.

Hysterectomy, however, is a major operation, whether associated with reassignment surgery or not, it has its own set of complications and problems with healing and recovery. Infection, blood loss, urinary difficulties and problems with bowel function are all to be considered and discussed with your surgeon, so that you are well informed. At all times, however, I believe the tubes and ovaries should be removed along with the uterus no matter what technique is planned.

Genital Reassignment Procedures

Preliminary thoughts - When a surgeon performs reassignment, he/she has a number of problems to solve in the creation of a sensate, functional and aesthetic phallus. He/she must discuss in detail what he/she is prepared to do for you. When discussing these procedures, several factors must be kept in mind:

1. Perineal and labial molding in order to make the genital region as authentic as possible is very important. The labia will be used to create a scrotum for placement of testicular prostheses and the female appearance must be erased.

2. The problem of forming an urethral extension must be solved as expertly as possible. Whether the new urethra will be formed by bladder, or vaginal wall tissue, or a part of a skin flap from the abdomen or the arm, or skin/muscle flaps from other donor sites, is something that your surgeon should have in-depth past experience with and be able to discuss it with you, in detail.

3. Some surgeons feel that in their skill and expertise, they can construct the phallus and connect it completely in a single stage. Others surgeons feel very convinced that several procedures must be done to accomplish success. In other words, in their approach to reassignment, the various steps are staged. In some surgeons' approaches, two surgical teams are used to carry out the multiple steps and a microsurgeon may be a part of one of these teams to accomplish the connections of arteries, veins and nerves in a much more precise way. This is something you must inquire about and learn in detail what your surgeon plans for you.

4. The overall technique of phalloplasty is at best most difficult for the patient and for the surgeon. While a core of well-trained and dedicated surgeons from all over the world are striving to lessen many problems that are associated with such a formidable task, many difficulties still remain to be solved. There are still problems to control in reference to lessening scar formation in donor sites, to eliminating wound disruption in the new phallus, and to avoid strictures and fistula in the new urethra.

The problem of accomplishing comfortable and effective erection still needs much more investigation. Because the overall surgical approach to reassignment is so complex, you must be prepared for the fact that you may have the need for anywhere from three to seven, on an average, hospital admissions for procedures, either to accomplish what is originally intended, or to solve complications that have arisen in the performance of these various techniques.

Female to male requests of their surgeons

When F-M transsexuals are asked what they want to achieve in reassignment surgery, the answers are very specific. While the surgeons' goals are important and have been described in the medical literature, only one study currently exists which considers what the F-M individual is looking to accomplish. The Free University Hospital of Amsterdam recently reported in the medical literature the data from 150 returned questionnaires and compilation of that information reveals the following:

- A scrotum, a glans penis and a penile shaft that is aesthetically appealing. The whole of the external genitalia appearance when either nude or in a tight swimsuit, must be authentic and convincing.

- The act of urination while standing is a primary goal, and urination should be as comfortable and free of problem as possible.

- Rigidity or erection by way of a technique that is comfortable and moderately easy to accomplish.

- A sensate genitalia is desired. This means not only to touch but erogenous sensation with penetration as well.

- There should be minimal disfigurement and no functional loss in the various donor sites.

These goals can be accomplished by the physician experienced and skilled in F-M assignment, but the techniques are challenging and formidable even in the most gifted of hands. As stated before, while some surgeons claim this whole reassignment technique can be a one-stage procedure, there are those who believe that a one-stage approach is not yet possible, and that several stages must be planned and executed. Certain complications can add to the number of procedures that may be needed to have full and successful reassignment. One encouraging thing that comes to mind as one reads this particular surgical literature is that there is a great amount of effort going into perfecting the operations. The surgeons contributing their experience and knowledge are very dedicated and very involved to solving the technical problems that still remain. The vast number of different surgical techniques described in the medical literature are a testament to the inventiveness and resourcefulness of these physicians. However, the great number of techniques described are also indicative of the great problems in accomplishing successful reassignment.

The Problems to be Solved in the Creation of the Urinary Tract.

1. ***The urinary tract from bladder to tip of the glans penis (the urethra)-*** The problems encountered in establishing a urethra which will function in an uncomplicated way are several and hinge on the fact that the female or native urethra is short and will not reach the urethra constructed within the new or neo-phallus. In all of the techniques that are currently used for lengthening the urethra, nothing is done to change the normal or native urethra as it extends from the base of the bladder to the outside just above the vagina. But once again, it must be lengthened and connection or anastomoses must be made with the new conduit or passage, constructed in the phallus. That tissue connection is called the Pars Fixa Urethra.

The questions we need answers for are these:

   A.   What will be the tissue used to make that connection?

   B.   How can one avoid a breakdown or disruption of the anasto moses of that tissue connection to the native urethra (called a fistula)

   C.   Can one avoid strictures, or narrow areas, in any part of the new or neo-urethra in its entire length?

The techniques to create the pars fixa urethra are of several types:

A. Pedicled flaps of bladder wall or vaginal wall (mucosa) are fashioned. Pedicled means that the blood supply is kept intact by a pedicle attachment. The flaps are "swung down", formed into tubes and then connected to the native urethra on the one end and to the phallic urethra on the other end, when this structure is in place for such a connection.

B. Flaps of skin taken from donor sites on the labia minora and skin at the vaginal opening (vestibule) are other methods of creating the urethral connection. Other donor sites are the abdominal wall, the inguinal area and the inner thigh.

C. Extensions of the skin which form the urethra within the neo-phallus, the donor sites for this being the forearm and the abdominal wall. This extension of skin, when so fashioned, only needs one connection, that is to the native urethra, for it is continuous through the phallus to the very tip of the new organ. This is the "tube within a tube" technique which is utilized so often in the creation of the neo-phallus, and it will be described in more detail when we discuss the creation of the phallus.

The uretha

Several points should be emphasized in this very brief discussion of the elongation of the urethra from the base of the bladder to the penile tip:

a. Fistula formation or a break in the connection of these segments of tissue thereby allowing urine leakage is a real problem. To begin with, the tissue to tissue connection is unnatural. Dissimilar tissues are sometimes joined together. Healing is not always complete. Hence, a fistula or hole can result with unnatural urine loss. This is a real problem and reoperation is needed for large fistula although periods of time might elapse in the hope that a small fistula will close spontaneously.

b. Strictures can develop. These are a narrowing in the caliber of the urethra and when they do take place anywhere along the newly constructed neo-urethra, though they most often form at connection sites (anastomoses), usually dilatation is sufficient to reduce these. Dilatation, however, may be repeated a number of times in order to reduce the narrowing in the urethral canal.

c. Diverticula or sac-like out pouches can develop leading to urine residuals and annoying uncontrolled small amounts of urine loss at times. Occasionally, larger urine residuals may be retained in a urethral segment whose caliber is wider than intended, once again, leading to troublesome urine loss. These are generally repairable, but again, another procedure is added to those already done.

d. Urine infections in the bladder can result from catheterization and instrumentation. While generally treatable with appropriate bacterial identification and antibiotic therapy, sometimes bladder infections become chronic and occasionally, the kidneys or upper urinary tract becomes involved. This can be serious and all care must be exercised not to allow this latter complication to take place.

e. Some surgeons will "prefabricate" or devise the urethral connection or pars fixa urethra in a single stage before the phallic portion of the reassignment takes place. A period of time will be allowed to elapse before the phallic stage is done. In some literature reports, that period of time may be as long as a year.

The creation of that portion of urethra that lies inside the neo-phallus will be discussed when we look at phallus construction itself.

The creation of a scrotum

An aesthetically acceptable bifid scrotum is not discussed greatly in the medical literature. Most surgeons will construct this part of the external neo-genitalia from the labia majora, though a few report experience using flaps from the groin area, the pubic and the inguinal regions. The bifid appearance can be accomplished by appropriate suturing to create a median raphe or central dividing line. This gives an authenticity to the appearance of the scrotum. A measure of experience has been reported in the medical literature with creation of this structure and the insertion of testicular prosthesis, often using silicone implants to give the appearance and texture of the genuine testes. The operation can be combined with the prefabrication of the pars fixa urethra or can be independent of any of the procedures for reassignment. The problems encountered in the operation have to do with infection and wound disruption in a small number of patients and implant expulsions or implant dislocation in another percentage of those operated. The greatest number of those operated are uncomplicated. A reoperation will be necessary for those who experience prosthesis expulsion or dislocation, however.

The creation of a new or neo-phallus

The goals to accomplish in construction of the phallus in the F-M individual are quite formidable.

a. The phallus itself should be formed and attached with microsurgical techniques that will insure proper connection of all structures that are necessary for its survival. Because this is such a formidable task, many surgeons feel that this is not a one-stage procedure.

b. The appropriate microsurgical technique must accomplish good arterial blood supply to maximize healing and minimize possibilities of wound disruption and breakdown in the healing. The nerve supply should be well connected to allow for both tactile and erogenous sensibility.

c. The neo-urethra contained in the neo-phallus should be competent and allow for directed and comfortable voiding. If possible, the opening at the tip of the penis should have the slit configuration when at rest and the round appearance when the urinary stream is in passage.

d. The neo-phallus should have an appropriate aesthetic appearance when either nude or when clothed. The glans should be, if at all possible, sculptured with a corona as seen in the genetic male. The size and caliber of the phallus should be appropriate to the person's torso, size and build and with enough bulk to tolerate insertion of a prosthetic stiffener for successful penetration, if this is desired.

e. As stated before, the donor site for the neo-phallus should have minimal scarring or disfigurement and no functional loss.

There are great number of techniques that have been devised to construct a neo-phallus. They are ingenious, each and every one, and great thinking and experimentation has taken place with many surgeons at work to accomplish this surgical procedure. The abundance of techniques suggests strongly that none is ideal. There is yet room for improvement and the surgeons are still applying imagination and expertise -- don't lose faith!

The frequently used techniques employ pedicled skin flaps from a variety of donor sites. By pedicled, it is meant that the flap remains attached to its blood and nerve supply and is swung into its new place with all of these structures intact. The abdomen, particularly the area beneath the umbilicus, is a very common donor site, but flaps can be taken from the thigh and the groin. These flaps are tubed, which means that they are made into a structure that resembles the cardboard that paper toweling is wrapped around. In some instances, a portion of that flap may be so fashioned as to create an additional tube, a tube-within-a-tube technique that allows for creation of the neo-phallus portion of the urethra within the larger tube, the neo-phallus. This length of neo-urethra is skin-lined, and if the surgeon does not choose to use this technique, he/she can place another skin-lined tube within the newly created neo-phallus, donated from another donor site. Other tissues are sometimes used. In some of the procedures, muscle is a part of the flaps utilizing either the abdominal rectus muscle or the gracilis muscle from the thigh. This contributes more bulk to the phallus so as to accommodate a stiffener should it be so desired. Needless to say, all of these alternatives and various techniques need careful planning to insure adequate blood and nerve supply and provide as many of the goals I have mentioned.

Some surgeons use free (non-pedicled) flaps and take them from a variety of anatomic sites. The most frequently harvested free flap donor site is the forearm. Other places on the arm may be donor sites for instance, different places on the upper arm are often times used for these free flaps. The deltoid area is an example. The groin also may be a contributing donor site as well. When these free flaps are to be used, the construction of the phallic urethra (which is called the pars pendulans) may be made of other tissue or it may be constructed as is often the case in the forearm free flap using a tube-within-a-tube technique.

The experience of your surgeon will dictate how that part of the procedure will be conducted. But, certain principles should be kept in mind for both the construction of the phallus neo-urethra and the phallus itself:

A. The donor site for both the phallus and the intraphallic neo-urethra should be as free of hair as is possible. If needed, electrolysis well before surgery is a very worthwhile consideration.

B. The microsurgical connections of blood supply and nerve supply for both the phallus and its urethra must be done with precision and skill. The line of anastomoses for these tissues must also be done with great care, for remember the phallic urethral connection with the pars fixa urethra, (that connection to the native urethra) must be done with skilled technique to minimize fistula or stricture formation. Some surgeons prefer not to make that connection until many weeks later, hence another surgical procedure may need to be done. Urination may not take place through the phallus for some time after the phallus is attached.

Possible and additional complications to these approaches have to do with tissue breakdown or necrosis, either partial or total with urinary tract infection or infection in the neo-phallus or the donor site. If a fistula develops anywhere along the neo-urethra, and it is small, it may heal spontaneously. If it is large, additional surgery may be necessary to accomplish closure.

The glans penis, the very end of the phallus, can be sculptured and made to look very authentic. It can be given the ridge-like appearance (corona) that the male penis has, but with healing and time, that appearance could disappear and the shaft will be uniform to the very end of the phallus. A number of techniques exist to try and avoid that loss of contouring and a technique of tattooing is being used by several European surgeons in order to bypass that particular problem. Tattooing does demarcate the glans area and gives somewhat more of an authentic appearance.

Metaidoioplasty

There is one technique that should be mentioned that utilizes none of the involved complicated approaches briefly discussed. This technique is called metaidoioplasty, and it does not require disturbance and disfigurement of the torso or extremities to accomplish. It is an approach to the testosterone stimulated clitoris. As you will remember, the clitoris may grow to as much as 6 cm. under the influence of testosterone. A surgical freeing, or unhooding of the clitoris is what is done in this procedure, leaving a very tactile, sensitive organ. However, the freed clitoris is too small for penetration. For the individual not requiring that function in sexual activity and not caring to stand to urinate or even have urinary passage though this pseudophallus, this is a very appropriate technique. The cost in time, money and perhaps heartache is totally avoided. Some may elect this procedure while waiting for more development and less complication in phallic construction as it now exists.

Obtaining erection and function in the new or neo-phallus

This is an area wherein there is scant medical literature reporting, though there is experience in the various surgical techniques described by some surgeons doing reassignment for the F-M individual. Indications are that everything being done to effect neo-phallus erection for penetration, falls far short of the ideal. The surgical techniques to obtaining rigidity are these:

Transplants of bone or cartilage - These are taken from various places in the F-M individual, for instance cartilage may be harvested from one of the ribs. Since they are not foreign tissue, they are not extruded or rejected, but resorption, curving and fracture lend to failure over time. In addition, the phallus is constantly erect which is difficult to conceal and could be an embarrassment.

Implants - These are mechanical devices of varying designs, but generally are hydraulic or non-hydraulic. Both can be placed in a special pocket or channel in the phallus created at the time of phalloplasty, or they can be placed secondarily by the F-M individual when there is need in that specially created space in the phallus. Hydraulic prostheses tend to have more mechanical failure than non-hydraulic. Both however, can erode through the neo-tissue, leading to infection and tissue breakdown in the neo-phallus.

Other devices - The phallus may be provided with an extra skin-lined tunnel for insertion of a vaculum. This is a mesh-like structure that is inserted in the donor flap that will be used in phalloplasty construction. Trans urethral stiffeners and even condoms tightly applied to increase venous congestion in the neo-phallus have been suggested and used as well, all of these with varying degrees of success and failure.

Natural tissue change - In some individuals, edema, fibrosis (stiffened tissue) and scarring may be adequate to allow for some stiffening and penetration. The results of this natural occurence is variable and may actually disappear in time.

Suffice it to say, this whole technique is some distance behind the reassignment surgery itself.

This is a very brief overview of the many techniques and reports made to the medical literature. For the individual who has some measure of medical experience or ability to interpret the medical literature, I refer you to excellent articles in medical journals which detail the various procedures and techniques. Those written by J. Joris Hage are particularly notable.

After surgery - the Acute or In-Hospital Convalescence - M-F/F-M

Preliminary Remarks

Some procedures are done in an out-patient facility under local anesthesia or a spinal form of anesthesia. When this is the case, some of the presurgical preparation mentioned before this may be eliminated. All of that preparation will certainly be the case, however, when you have a general anesthetic. Your "awakening" from the procedure whether in-patient or out-patient will be in a recovery area where you will remain for an indefinite period of time, until you are stable enough and awake enough to be brought back to your room or go home. You will have all sorts of feelings and sensations. You may have a catheter in your bladder which gives you a feeling of pressure in the lower abdomen and an intense need to want to empty your bladder. If packing has been placed, this pressure feeling will be intensified. Your vital signs will be monitored by a very well trained nurse, and when appropriate in the recovery process, you may ask for pain medication. The intravenous placed before surgery, in the vein, will still be in, and you will feel mouth dryness and varying amounts of discomfort. Take courage - you won't be in this area for long.

Once back in your room - M-F/F-M

There will be pain and occasional nausea and vomiting. These are unfortunate aftermaths to anesthesia and the surgical procedure that you have experienced. Your floor nurses will have orders from your doctor for medications to be given for relief. They are generally on an "ask for" basis. DO ASK FOR THEM.

For a time, you will be confined to bed with no allowance to use the bathroom. The dressings for pressure and wound cover will be a nuisance, and if there is provision for drainage from the wound (a drain) or some spontaneous drainage soiling the dressings, this will be uncomfortable. Ask your nurse for changes or added dressings as the case may be. If you have an indwelling catheter in the bladder, it will drain urine from the bladder, relieving you of that bother, but it may feel uncomfortable and often gets in the way. Your intravenous fluids will be kept in place until you can take fluids adequately by mouth, or it may be necessary to leave it in place for delivery of special medication, particularly antibiotics. GRIN AND BEAR IT. It is very necessary for as long as it is in place. You may have elastic hose placed on your legs to lessen the possibilities of developing phlebitis. The hosiery will be changed periodically and you should move your legs and feet often in bed to keep venous blood moving up from the legs, into the venous system in your body.

All of these things are a part of the immediate postoperative recovery. Dependent upon what procedures have been done, you will soon be out of bed, free of tubes and IV lines, excreting on your own and taking a normal diet. Various surgical procedures have different requirements and prohibitions in the postoperative convalescence and surgeons impose their own views and preferences as well. In addition, the patient's response to pain, annoyance and varying degrees of apprehension and adaptability all influence the postoperative phase. Suffice it to say you **will** recover and you **will** move through this uncomfortable time. In the latter part of your convalescence, packing will be removed and replaced, or done away with altogether. Dressings will be discarded and bodily functions will all come back to normal.

Potential problems in the acute/hospital convalescence - M-F/F-M

What your physician, your nursing staff and you desire, in addition to the completion of a successful surgical procedure, is an uncomplicated postoperative convalescence. For many it will be so. For a few, some problems can develop. They must be anticipated by your medical team, or if they are not anticipated and do occur, they must be quickly recognized and treated. Your hospital stay will be influenced by the ease with which you recover, and if any complications develop, the ease and competence with which they are managed.

A. **Prior medical conditions** - If you have hypertension, or if you have diabetes, or if there is any other preexisting medical concerns that might be altered by your surgical experience, these will be provided for by your surgeon in the postoperative orders that are given to the recovery room nursing staff, and then to the floor nurses. These will have been reviewed in detail with you and will have been a part of the information shared with your surgeon by the at **home medical physician**. Whatever your medications preoperative for those medical conditions (not your hormones - remember these will have been interrupted), they will be given to you by vein or muscle injection until you can assume your own self medication regimen as it was before the operation.

B. **Postoperative infection** - It is unfortunate that humans are subject to infection, and it all depends on the virulence of the offending pathogen and the host susceptibility. In a surgical experience and in the acute convalescence from the procedure, you are susceptible. It has little to do generally with operating techniques, we presume they are always optimal for avoiding operative infection. Infection, however, does happen, and it can manifest itself in several ways.

1. *The lungs* - Subsequent to anesthesia when you are put completely to sleep, the lungs may undergo mild collapse in the peripheral areas. This is called atelectasis. Infection can develop in these collapsed

areas. Special procedures are utilized to limit and curtail the problem. Postoperative breathing techniques with special machines and inspiratory exercises may be ordered along with antibiotic therapy if the process is too progressive. You are wise to breathe and exhale deeply five or six times on your own, every waking hour or so for the first 48 hours after surgery. This minimizes the development of this unfortunate problem. Individuals with preexisting lung problems, particularly smokers, are real candidates for this difficulty.

2. *The urinary tract* - The manipulation of the lower urinary tract (the urethra and the bladder) in surgical procedures and the placement of a catheter which may be indwelling for some few days, makes the potential for urinary tract infection all too possible. Bacteria introduced to the bladder has potential to ascend the ureter on one or both sides and involve the upper urinary tract (the kidneys). This is very much a problem. Any pre-existing urinary tract problems can make this potential even more a probability. If in the postoperative period, either with a catheter in place or not, should fever and chills, along with lower abdominal pain or lower back pain develop, these complaints must be investigated with blood culture, urine cultures and blood counts, along with evaluation of other potential sites for infection. If you are urinating spontaneously, you may develop a sense of frequency or an urgent need to void and a sense of burning when you do void. These are other symptoms indicating that the urinary tract is the focus for investigation and treatment. The blood cultures will indicate whether or not the blood has become infected as well. This sometimes does take place, and the urinary and blood cultures will identify the bacterial organism, so that specific antibiotics can be selected to eliminate this problem. Urinary tract infections usually respond quickly and completely to appropriate antibiotics. Occasionally a chronic problem develops, and more involved investigation will be necessary. Every effort must be made to avoid upper tract infection, and if it takes place, there should be a great deal of effort to treat it fully and be sure that no focus of infection remains with post treatment urine cultures.

3. *The wound and donor sites* - Once our skin is interrupted or opened, bacteria will enter our bodies. Our natural defenses can help notably to limit spread of the infection, but those defenses can fail and the infection can progress to involve our whole body and all of its systems. Hence, the infection can be either localized or systemic. Whatever the case, the wound site should be cultured for the offending bacteria and antibiotic therapy initiated appropriately. Once culture reports are available from the laboratory, your surgeon may change the antibiotic regime or intensify it, according to your clinical condition. Wound and donor site infections can disrupt the surgical wound,

and occasionally with intensive infections, the operated area could breakdown or heal differently than intended by the surgeon. Sometimes infection becomes quite localized and an infection collection (abscess) may need to be opened and drained to accomplish cure. A variety of approaches are available to your doctor depending upon how effectively you and your antibiotic regime fight this unfortunate complication.

4. *Phlebitis and pulmonary embolism* - When the veins in the lower extremities or the pelvic area of the abdomen become inflamed, we speak of this as phlebitis. This process can take place in the superficial or deep venous systems of the legs, and if clotting mechanism changes accompany this inflammatory condition, particularly in the deep veins of the legs, or in the major veins of the pelvis, then clots form and attach themselves to the vein walls (thrombosis). If these clots break away, they will travel in the venous system to the right side of the heart and subsequently to the lungs. (This is called pulmonary embolism.) This is a most concerning problem, for depending upon the degree of embolism and the places where these clots may lodge in the lungs, we can have a very sick person, or possibly even risk death. Once phlebitis is diagnosed, very vigorous treatment is initiated. Anticoagulation with blood thinners is begun and may be continued for months thereafter. Hormonal therapy which would be ordinarily reinstituted at appropriate time after convalescence, will not be started for some great length of time, if ever. This is a serious complication. **Remember, your hormone therapy must be interrupted a good four to six weeks before your surgery.** No matter how you feel physically without it -- no matter how deprived you feel emotionally by not being able to take it, this short period of time is nothing compared to a postoperative lifetime without your hormones. With the development of phlebitis and/or embolism, this could be the case. All measures to avoid development of phlebitis and its consequences, should be discussed with your surgeon before your operation.

C. **Bowel function disturbance** - Whenever the abdomen is entered and/or the bowel is handled, a condition called paralytic ileus can result and usually does. In simple terms, the small and large bowel "shut down" - nothing moves through these areas of bowel, and gas accumulates, causing abdominal distention and discomfort. The condition can clear spontaneously and actually does most often. Occasionally, the problem intensifies and obstructive problems must be ruled out. There are a variety of ways to manage an ileus, particularly one that does not resolve rather quickly. Nasogastric tubes, intravenous fluids and strict prohibition of food and drink by mouth may be the approaches instituted, should this problem develop. Those having surgery with no entry to the abdomen will generally not experience this complication to any degree. Those who have a colovaginoplasty (wherein large bowel is used to form the neo-vagina) have a good chance of encountering this condition.

Sometimes the return of bowel function is just sluggish and slow. You can rely on your nurse to inquire generally about bowel function. Don't avoid any help needed or offered in either laxatives, rectal suppositories or possibly an enema or two. You want to reestablish all body systems to as near as you experienced it before your surgery.

D. **The return of urinary function** - Once the catheters are removed and urine begins to flow without a hint of retention or infection, you will be in a much happier state. But, be sure that you feel comfortable with your voiding habits. Remember, the instrumentation of the bladder can lead to infection problems when out of the hospital and once back at home. Discuss with your doctor the possibility of a "clean catch" sample of urine being sent to the hospital laboratory before your discharge from the hospital. This helps to determine that no bacteria are there to cause problems with infection at a later time.

Occasionally, the bladder is dysfunctional and it works improperly. It may have spasm or it may retain a volume of urine after each voiding. If prolonged catheterization is needed because of dysfunction, you may be sent home with a catheter in place. Be sure you discuss adequately with your surgeon what instructions he wants you to follow, what he wants your physician at home to do for you, and whether it is feasible to take antibiotics during the time the catheter is indwelling. Be sure this information is transmitted by your operating surgeon to your physician at home (it should be a part of your discharge summary).

Special considerations for the Male to Female individual - M-F

Neo-vaginal dilatation - Once the packing has been removed from the vagina, you will be given instructions for the technique of dilatation. This is a very important task. Surgeons differ on how they want you to dilate, or what to use, and for how long. You should be very clear on what your doctor intends for you and follow those instructions as closely as you can. It will be uncomfortable at first, but your attentiveness to the task and your strong adherence to the proper routine will insure for later, a functional and comfortable vagina. And prepare you very adequately for sexual activity as you intend to experience it. You will change the size of your dilators. Do this with care and over appropriate time. You will be advised to use a lubricant, available over-the-counter at your pharmacy. K-Y Jelly or Surgilube are good materials to use. In several weeks, you could consider using estrogen vaginal cream as prescribed by your physician. Placing this on the dilator and into the vagina will be very good for the walls of the neo-vagina, aiding in its pliability.

An effective dilating plan that many surgeons advise is to use two dilators for an extended period of time -- one of smaller caliber for 10 minutes, the slightly larger one for 15-20 minutes just after. This double placement consumes about one-half hour of time and should start about 1 - 1 1/2 hours after completion of the last dilation experience. To dilate about 6 times a day for 3-6 months will be necessary. Very gradual increase in the caliber of each dilator is to be encouraged. Your gynecologist caring for you in your **late** convalescence can advise you of your progress and the size of the dilators to use. Keep in mind that the goal is for comfortable, penetrative sexual activity when your healing is complete. Proper dilation will insure caliber and depth of the neovagina. In the absence of sexual intercourse, dilation about twice a day will be imperative for a year or more for some.

Douching - There will be no place for this technique for some weeks after your surgery, unless there is such a notable amount of drainage that your physician wants you to douche. Generally, I would suggest that you not begin this approach until some time later in your convalescence. We will discuss this hygienic approach in the third section of the book. You should be aware that douches can be purchased over-the-counter at your pharmacy, and that they are made of different substances. Be sure to ask your doctor what he/she intends for you at this particular time and when he/she wants you to start.

Sexual Relations - The very best neo-vaginal dilator is the penis, but you may not be inclined to consider this, and if you are, you probably should not engage in penetrative sex for about three months after your surgical procedure. Your dilatation will be very appropriate and helpful as long as you follow the proper routine. Sexual intercourse could be too forceful and potentially injurious if attempted before that three month interval has passed.

Special considerations for the Female to Male individual - F-M

If you are to experience a single-stage phalloplasty procedure, wherein the urinary tract and the neo-phallus are created in one surgical experience, your need to know certain things will differ from that individual having reassignment divided into several stages. Assuming that no complication arises, you will be given instructions upon discharge. Those instructions will be detailed and they should be **in print** for your easy reference.

Your doctor's orders for you should center upon several special areas:

The urinary tract - If the pars fixa urethra is unconnected to a phallus urethra, certain things must be kept in mind. To begin with, you have an actual extension of your own urethra. For a time after this was created in surgery, you may have had a catheter through the urethral tract, or you may have had a suprapubic catheter (a "hole" in the top of the bladder made through the abdominal wall where a special catheter assists urinary passage.)

This latter technique allows healing at the neo-urethral anastomosis or union. You will need your surgeon's instructions to care for that neo-urethra and for the suprapubic catheter site, for whatever time will elapse with catheterization. Drink fluids liberally and include cranberry juice daily to help avoid infection, for remember that is a very possible complication.

If the neo-urethra is connected to the pars pendulans - the phallic urethra, you may or may not have a catheter for a period of time. Make inquiry of your surgeon about catheter care instructions - how and when to flush the catheter -- how and when to remove it! Is urine culture necessary to do when the catheter comes out? (I think it is!) Should you be on a prophylactic antibiotic to lessen the chances of post-catheter urinary tract infection? (I think there are very notable times when this is the proper approach.)

The care of the neo-phallus - There will be a suture line on the shaft of the penis (hopefully the under surface.) Who will be the person to remove these sutures if they are to be taken out? Is there any particular care to be given if drainage develops in the suture line or from the meatus or opening at the tip of the neo-phallus? What should you look for in the healing of the phallic attachment to the pubic region of your abdomen? How soon will a visit be scheduled to see your operating surgeon for follow up or will you be seen for care by your surgeon at home? These are important questions to ask and to be clarified completely before you leave your operating surgeon's care.

The care of the donor site - Donor sites may be the arm (it should be the least dominant arm) the abdomen, the buttocks or the thighs. When the donor site for phallus construction is full thickness and includes tissue below the full thickness graft, to some depth, a graft from another site will be needed to close that first donor site. These will need attention and your instructions should include all specifics for your successful healing and all guidelines to help you bring poor healing and/or infection to the attention of your **'at-home' surgeon** quickly. It must be said, again, that your **'at home' surgeon** will absolutely require written data and information from the operating surgeon of all the primary surgery and donor sites. Information must be sent to that **'at home' surgeon** as to what you experienced when your reassignment procedure was performed. Certain techniques or instructions should be made known to you and to your **'at home' surgeon** to aid healing and avoid infection problems.

Discharge from the hospital - M-F/F-M

The length of hospital stay is directly related to the procedure and your ability to recover without incident, or if complication develops, its complete resolution. When you are ready to go, several points must be stressed.

Who will come for you? Arrange to have someone to transport you to your interim living facility. Hopefully, you will have been able to arrange such that they will stay with you. You will need help. No matter how you fared in the hospital setting, your strength and reserves will be limited, and at times you will feel as if you have been hit "with a sour apple."

Where will you go? I mentioned an interim residence previously, and with purpose. If at all possible, you should try to stay at a comfortable place near to your surgeon, hopefully until it is decided when you should have your first post-operative evaluation. This gives the operating surgeon opportunity to view the progress of healing, and to review with you what you are experiencing. This makes for more continuity in your care. It also allows your operating surgeon to forward additional information and instruction to your 'at home' surgeon/physician. You will profit from that additional time spent recovering near your operating doctor.

What will you be told?

You should insist on:

a. Written instruction with specific attention to any instructions regarding complications that may have arisen during your in-hospital stay. These are for your own use.

b. Written instructions for your physicians at home and that includes your medical doctor and your surgeon. Both should receive by mail, or hand carry, the following:

       1. A discharge summary.
       2. Pertinent laboratory data.
       3. The operative report.
       4. Discussion of postoperative complications and suggestions for follow up care.

c. Prescriptions for appropriate medications. This will include antibiotics, sedatives, medication for sleep if needed, and certainly medication for pain. Your surgeon will advise you as to when it will be appropriate for you to recommence your hormonal therapy. Actually, what hormonal regimen you used before surgery may be revised once you are at home with your medical physician. Your surgeon should not assume the task of assigning a medical regime or revising that which you used formerly. This is in the prerogative of your at home doctor.

Your at home physicians can best serve you if they are informed. In my opinion, it is essential that you make arrangement for all information to be exchanged with these doctors **before** you have surgery, wherever it is to take place.

Back at Home - M-F

Schedule to see your physicians shortly after you arrive home. The first physician to see is your surgeon. Hopefully, he/she will have received instructions from the operating doctor, and he/she will want to review with you the surgical procedure and evaluate your progress. Sutures may need to be removed from various operative sites. Healing may be optimal, but there may also be need for various kinds of help from your **at home surgeon**. He/she should have access to the operating surgeon for discussion in event of problems. Once all details are looked after, you should then schedule with your **medical doctor** to evaluate your general health and your need for any special testing or medical care. Your hormonal regime will need review as well. Generally M-F individuals can have a reduction in their presurgical regimen. It may be comfortable to do this from the start of the new routine, but then again it may not, and adjustments can be made easily as time goes on. For F-M individuals, usually the same regimen will be needed, but your doctor's experience and your responses will be guidelines for you both.

Ordinarily, routine blood hormone evaluations are not necessary in either individual just after surgery. Testing for blood lipids, liver evaluations and other areas of concern, must be continued as indicated by what your medical physician knows of your health status and what your transgendered health modifications have imposed upon you. Later, yearly testing will be scheduled. All of the appropriate habits are still to be looked at carefully and seriously. You still need to watch diet and weight and other health concerns (i.e., smoking, drinking, etc.) but you have passed a very significant milestone. You are now whole and entirely one in body and mind -- and it's time to move on to your life thereafter.

D - THE LATE CONVALESCENCE AND LIFE THEREAFTER

The late convalescence - M-F/F-M

In the late convalescence, that period of time from your return home from the hospital to your resumption of full activity, certain considerations are common for both the M-F and the F-M individual.

Depending upon the type of surgery and depending on lack of complication in hospital recovery, you may have a measure of discomfort of varying degree and some disruption of adequate bowel and bladder function. You may have weakness. Infections treated in the hospital may once again recur, especially in the operative or donor sites, or in the urinary tract. Bacteria are always with us, even with strictest precaution and good technique in the hospital during and after surgery. With high resistance on your part and low virulence on the part of the offending organism, infection may not be a recurring difficulty for you. Yet with changes that are not expected in drainage from the operative or donor areas (that is in color, or amount, or odor) your doctor at home should be notified and an office visit might be in order. Problems with urination, such as pain, frequency, a sense of urgent need to empty the bladder, or any change that is not the usual or what you have experienced as ordinary, should be reported as well. Fever and chills are very real reasons to speak to your interim surgeon. A change in the ability to eat, the development of nausea and vomiting, or adverse bowel changes such as diarrhea, are again reason to discuss what you are experiencing with your physician. As we have noted before, your physician will have information sent to him by your operating surgeon and there may be the need to arrange to see that doctor at a time earlier than previously planned.

There is no doubt that as time goes by, you will feel stronger, eat more comfortably and be free of annoyances in body function. Certain things however, specific to your genital reassignment surgery, could develop and you should be alert to their possibility.

General Comments on Home care - M-F/F-M

On your return home from the hospital, you will have varying degrees of discomfort and different activity and energy levels. Tolerance for surgical insult and responses vary so much from one to another. It is very hard to predict or even to cover all potentials for what one may encounter in the first few weeks at home. That is why your arrangement for having a surgeon available to you on your return is exceedingly important.

Here are a few precepts to consider and to incorporate into your daily regimen:

Take your medications - Take them on time if a time schedule is given to you. Take them when needed, for instance, pain medication should not be avoided or delayed, and you should follow the instruction for pain relief as given to you by your physician. If you are given antibiotics or you have special medications for specific medical concerns, take them as you are instructed. Take your hormones as prescribed by your **medical physician** and not your surgeon. Occasionally, surgeons change hormones and dosage. This in my view is not appropriate unless some interchange has taken place with the surgeon and the medical physician allowing for that change.

Drink a great deal of water - **at least 6-8 large glasses per day** - This tends to dilute the urine. In each day there should be included in your fluid intake, 2-3 glasses of cranberry juice to help "sterilize" the urine. Drinking a great deal sometimes causes urinary frequency and this should not be confused with the possibility of infection. Keep your bladder functioning to bring back stable, normal function and to make evident early, any improper function of the urinary tract. You are not to experience burning or urgency with urination, nor incontinence, dribbling, or evidence of urinary bladder retention (infrequent voiding or no voiding.) Reporting these complaints to the interim surgeon is very important.

Instructions regarding wound care - Your surgeon will have given you certain precautions and activities regarding the operated area. Donor sites will need dressings and sometimes application of medicine, along with watchfulness against trauma and signs of infection.

In the M-F individual, the newly created vagina will have discharge. The character and an estimate of how much to expect should be told to you. Variations may need reporting. Dilation should be discussed with you in detail, the timing, the kind and size of dilator, and the length of time for use, all should be familiar to you and a plan for the progression in this activity should be quite clear in your mind.

In the F-M individual, the penis and extended urethra will need special attention. Surgical scars will need cleansing and protection. The instructions your operating surgeon gave to you should be a part of the information sent along to your interim surgeon. Your operating surgeon perhaps will have specific instructions which he favors, and you should be prepared to follow them closely. When things don't seem to be progressing adequately, contact should be made with your operating surgeon if the problem seems major, but in most instances, contact with the interim surgeon will be appropriate. Occasionally as I have indicated, there is need to speak with both of them. They may need to talk to each other as well about accurate diagnosis and management of certain problems.

For the M-F individual - Douching will likely be out of the question for a time and you shouldn't attempt it unless you have full allowance and instruction from your interim surgeon. Some of the details to know regarding douching will be discussed a little further on.

Specific late convalescent concerns for the Male to Female - M-F

The following problems generally become evident once you are recovering at home:

Fistula formation - A fistula is a passage formed in the healing process, between structures that should not be connected. Fistulas take place for a variety of reasons, sometimes single or in combination. Suffice it to say, they defy ordinary body function. For the postoperative M-F individual, the possibilities are fistulous connections between the vagina and the bladder, or the vagina and the rectum. A fistula could form between the urethra and vagina, though this is less common. A fistulous tract could form between any of these organs, the neovagina, the bladder, the rectum and the skin.

Fistulas developing between the bladder and the vagina are evident when the postoperative individual experiences urine loss through the vagina. Rectovaginal fistulas are evident when fecal waste is noted coming from the vagina. In either instance, the fistulous opening may be small or quite large. Spontaneous closure, or natural healing, is more possible with small fistulas and more apt to take place with communications between bladder and vagina. Large fistulas and fistulas that develop between the rectum and vagina often do not close or heal over spontaneously, and must be operated upon. Both are very great inconveniences and will be left for a time before surgical closure is attempted. This leads to great disruption in the convalescence and the ability to return to normal activities. The management of these fistulas will be dependent on size and anatomic location of the tract, and great patience is needed to put up with the problem while waiting for its resolution. Some fistulas between bowel and vagina could result in a temporary colostomy while planning repair.

Neovaginal slough - If the neovagina, all or a part of it, loses its viability through loss of blood supply, regardless of what it is formed of (penile skin, scrotum or skin flaps from other donor sites,) it will "die" and the tissue will slough out causing a disruption or defect in the new vagina. This can lead to a need for reconstruction of the vagina since the tendency for scarring or narrowing is very great with this late complication. This could prompt consideration of the colovaginoplasty procedure for repair.

Neovaginal prolapse - If the neovagina becomes detached or separated from the walls of the tunnel that were developed for the new vaginal lining, the vagina will then protrude. It will invaginate to a greater or lesser extent and appear like a sock turned inside out. Some surgeons use approaches in their technique to avoid this complication, and while it is not a common one, it does necessitate reoperation should it occur. The repair may be to reattach the prolapsed organ if possible to do so, however, it may require complete reconstruction of a new vagina.

Compromised urinary habits - This complication may take any number of forms, from incontinence to urinary retention, in varying degrees. Chronic bladder infection may develop or frequent acute infections of the urinary tract may take place. The need for cultures to identify bacteria and to treat with specific antibiotics is very important and your doctor should do this with very little delay. Altered urinary stream direction may be noted, or a spraying of urine may take place as urine exits from the external urethral opening. There may be need to alter the sitting position to direct urine into the commode. This is a great annoyance and very unnatural. All of these are generally due to placement of the urethra inappropriately and must be dealt with accurately to correct the defective function. Cystoscopy and intravenous pyelograms and even ultrasound study may be a part of the evaluation, especially with more chronic or persistent urinary complaint. This set of problems must be corrected as completely as is possible. Your doctor must not just treat this difficulty in a casual way.

Vaginal stenosis - Vaginal dilatation, when indicated, is so very important. The natural tendency of a newly created vagina is to close at the external opening but, in fact, can narrow anywhere in it's length. There can also be some measure of shortening of the new vagina. Dilatation as instructed, and even for a time beyond the anticipated need, is a very definite part of the convalescence. Your instruction is given to you before you are discharged from the hospital and your first experience with dilatation should take place before leaving in the presence of your physician as he or she encourages and instructs you. Technique for continued and progressive dilatation should be outlined to you and carried out by you with no relaxation in your resolve to perform this task. When sexual relations are allowed to you, the best dilator, the penis, will continue to insure the continued proper patency of the neovagina. Often in the initial process with metal or plastic dilators, the discomfort is great enough to discourage the newly operated person to a point of abandoning the dilatory procedure. This is a mistake. Talking with the primary surgeon or the interim physician about ways to lessen the discomfort through appropriate lubrication is important. The use of pain medication can help greatly to lessen the discomfort. Ask for a prescription. More gradual increase in dilator size will be a part of the plan in time. This is very appropriate conversation with your physician, and I urge you not to stop the dilatation.

Urethral stenosis - The urethra may develop a degree of closure most often at the external opening, not the opening to the bladder. This will lead to various urinary discomforts. Altered urinary stream direction, urine retention in the bladder, bladder infections and other urine excretory problems will accompany the gradual change in the urethral caliber. You should report changes in urinary function as early as you are aware of them, for this can lead to prompt diagnosis and ready treatment. Generally, these urethral problems are solvable when proper diagnosis is made.

Specific late convalescent concerns for the Female to Male - F-M

Special problems can develop for the F-M person after surgery once having returned home. Most will be evident in the weeks before return to full activity and work. Several could develop at a much later date, however.

Fistula formation - A fistula is a passage formed, during the healing process, between structures that should not be connected. A fistulous tract will develop for a variety of reasons, sometimes one or several in combination. Suffice it to say that they defy the usual body function and the intent of your surgeon. For the F-M individual, the most common locations for fistulous tracts are at the connections where neourethral segments are united. In our discussion about neourethral construction, we spoke of the union of the pars urethra fixa to the native urethra at one end, and to the phallic urethra at the other end. These places can weaken in the healing, and the urinary stream can break through the weakened place to emerge through the phallic skin along the shaft, or at the junction of the phallus to the lower abdominal wall. These generally need surgical repair, for spontaneous closure may not take place readily. When this very unfortunate problem makes itself known, you must notify both the operating surgeon and the interim surgeon. Many precautions are taken in the primary surgical procedure, whether it be single or multiple stage, to avoid this complication. It is really a serious problem when it happens. Your inconvenience is great and the delay in returning to expected and normal activity is notable. This complication does not mean incompetence in your surgeon. It does happen unfortunately in a few individuals.

Donor site wound infection, disruption and scarring - Whether free or pedicled flaps or grafts are used for phallic or scrotal construction, there is always the danger of infection and/or wound disruption in the healing process. Some scarring will always accompany healing even without infection or wound separation. The hope is that it will be as little as possible. When infection and wound edge separation takes place, healing is interrupted and even when those problems are managed successfully, scarring could be more extensive. Any drainage or wound separation that does not appear appropriate, must be reported to the interim surgeon. Likely he/she will want to look at the problem and then institute appropriate therapy. He/she may need to contact the operating surgeon as well.

Phallus infection and/or tissue slough - As previously noted, the phallus is formed from grafts, free or pedicled, of thick skin. It can become infected, and if the infection is severe enough and extends to the suture line on the penile shaft, the neopenis tissue may undergo slough or tissue death with loss of its esthetic appearance and function. This can be limited to a very small area or could involve the entire neophallus. The degree of infection and loss of tissue viability may be something managed completely by the interim surgeon. This complication must be reported to both surgeons and a visit to the primary surgeon may be an eventuality.

Compromised urinary habits - The most common complication is urinary tract infection, and early identification of the bacteria and appropriate treatment is very important. Other potential problems may be incontinence, or residual urine collections in the bladder or in the new urethra, leading to dribbling, or delayed, or interrupted emptying. Calculi or stone formation in areas where sutures have not completely dissolved, is also a potential.

Urethral stenosis or closure - At places where the different urethral segments are joined or sutured, scarring can take place, leading to narrowing or stenosis. These are called strictures. Actually, stenotic areas can be found anywhere along the entire urethral length, from bladder to the tip of the neophallus. Changes in urinary stream caliber, and/or signs of infection, can be due to urethral narrowing or stricture.

Extrusion of erection devices and testicular implants - In time no matter what technique is used for accomplishing erection, there is the potential for tissue breakdown and expulsion of the stiffener or inflatable device. The ability to devise the ideal stiffening technique and have it function without complication is not as yet a reality.

Office visits in the late convalescence - M-F/F-M

We have talked of the need to have appropriate at-home medical and surgical physicians available to you on your return home. The services of the medical physician and surgeon may overlap for a time. The interim surgeon will serve generally only until you are fully healed and functional, and while that is usually the time until you return to full activity, sometimes this period might extend a bit longer dependent upon the difficulty.

In the usual sequence of things however, it is reasonable to call several days after your return to schedule a visit with the **at home surgeon** for about 7-10 days later. He/she will have received information about you, and he/she will apply it to your stage of recovery at that time. Sutures may need to be removed. The degree of healing, the absence of problem in the operated areas and the absence of concerning complaints are what he or she will be interested in, in their evaluation of you. Advice will be given and the interim surgeon should send a letter to your operating surgeon to complete the informational circle. The primary surgeon will appreciate knowing you are progressing well. It is also important to let your medical physician have a copy of that letter.

The second visit should be scheduled as is indicated by the first visit. In general, a two week interval would be reasonable, and your instructions relative to activity, special procedures, medication and possibly dietary concerns should be quite clear to you. By the time of the second visit, healing will be quite advanced and your activities will be measurably increased. Much of your medication other than hormones and the usual medicines for those aspects of health that are specific to you, will be a thing of the past. After that second visit, in the absence of problems, you should be able to plan your return to work and it should be discussed with your doctor. There should also be discussion about increasing your activity, about sexual involvements, strenuous exercise and douching for the M-F, and when these different considerations may be allowed. Again with all being normal and acceptable to your surgeon and yourself, you may not be scheduled for a revisit. Appointment for a visit will then be scheduled with your medical physician. However, that will depend fully on the extent of your surgery and the degree of healing.

Visits with your medical physician from this time forward will likely be infrequent as well. The first should be arranged for just before or just after the one month surgeon visit. At that visit, your medical doctor should have information from the operating surgeon and the interim surgeon to review with you. He/she may or may not want to examine your surgical results. He/she should review with you your hormonal regimen with a view to possibly lowering your hormonal medications dosage. (This is particularly the case with the M-F individual.) Once surgery is completed, you generally don't need as much in the way of maintenance medication. He/she should conduct the visit as a routine monitoring visit with not as much in-depth examination or inquiry as he/she would on a yearly visit. The laboratory studies that he will order will be as are indicated. But, all that depends upon your general health status and any medical needs arising since you met with him/her before surgery. There may be discussion about urinary habits, vaginal hygiene and dilatation for the M-F and penile and scrotal care in the F-M. If no revisit in the near future is planned, then a six-month revisit schedule is appropriate. Eventually your visits may not be anymore often than once a year for a general health evaluation and laboratory study, unless you have special problems that need evaluation more often.

For M-F and the F-M individual - Sexual activity is on hold until complete healing is accomplished and functionality of the new genitalia is established.

There is no doubt that in a few weeks after returning home, you will be moderately active. You will be shopping, going out to lunch and to dinner, visiting family and friends and involving yourself in a number of ways before returning to work. The degree of activity will be very unique to you, your level of recovery and your energy and your reserve.

Be sure you are ready for your return to the workplace. Discussion about this, with details about your work fully explored with your interim surgeon, is quite important. Once you return to work and its full schedule, you should be very ready for it. To go back into a convalescence sometimes is necessary with the development of a notable complication, but when things have gone smoothly and appropriately for you, you want to be sure that you are ready to assume your full work activities. Unreal expectations and inappropriate planning can prove difficult for you and your employer, and it could jeopardize your health and your job status.

Life Thereafter - M-F/F-M

There are some suggestions that I make to you, both the M-F and F-M individual, that just make good sense, now that your surgery is behind you, now that you have integrated yourself into society and you are building, growing, and enjoying family, friends, and perhaps a special someone. You cannot forget about your good health and its preservation. To begin with, make it a definite, each and every year to have a complete physical examination. It should include appropriate blood profile and testing as is indicated or necessitated by medical problems specific to you.

In addition, have a definite exercise program and stick to it. We all profit from appropriate exercising. Whatever is right for you in your need to control your eating habits and to be knowledgeable about calories, cholesterol intake and weight management is vastly important. Doesn't it make good sense? Whatever is necessary for you to maintain good health is all important. Sensible use of alcohol and putting aside the habit of smoking is also to be stressed. There is no way of getting around it, smoking is not good for you. I don't want to appear to be hounding you to consider good sensible living habits, but knowledgeable plans for preserving your health and extending your life, make your existence one of quality.

Specific thoughts for the
Male to Female in daily living - M-F

Your hormone therapy must be continued - Some individuals believe that once completing surgery, there is no further use of hormones and are willing to abandon estrogen in particular. This is not true. You need estrogen more now than before the removal of the large source of testosterone that you once had. You need it for preservation of your bones. Osteoporosis can develop without your hormonal therapy. Proneness to fractures increases with increasing osteoporosis. Hence, if only for this reason as well as continuing the preservation of the feminizing effect, you must continue using your estrogen. The dosage may be lower than before surgery, but its great value is supported by investigation done by experienced researchers in transgendered medicine.

Medical Issues

There is also the knowledge that estrogen continues to protect your heart and blood vessels. Hence, once more, to stop it would place you in the position of developing cardiovascular disease much more rapidly and at an earlier age. This means a lifelong use of your estrogen medication, it's true, but as you can see, the medication is very valuable. Other medicines may be necessary for your continued good health. You should always continue to observe what you are instructed by your medical physician in regard to those medications.

On a daily basis, it is a very good idea to take one adult aspirin tablet. It tends to modify the coagulation system in your blood and that helps greatly against clot formation in the veins (thrombophlebitis) and in the arteries (occlusion of the coronary or heart vessels). Some people feel strongly about use of vitamins, and in appropriate and sensible doses, I offer no objection, though with balanced and planned diet, their need may not be that absolute.

Vaginal care is important - You will have discharge no matter what surgical procedure was done for you. Good hygienic care is important. You accomplish this in several ways.

1. Douching
2. Vaginal lubrication
3. Estrogen creams (i.e. Premarin, Estrace or Ogen)

The value of douching - The pH or the acid/alkaline ratio of the vagina in the genetic female is slightly more acid than alkaline. This promotes the growth of a normal bacterial inhabitant in the vagina called lactobacillus. When infections take place and/or pH is disturbed, lactobacillus growth is interfered with and reestablishing the correct bacterial population and the correct pH can be a difficulty. Douches can do several things:

a. Reestablish the proper pH
b. Allow for adequate lactobacillus growth to take place.
This will establish proper pH and promotion of lactobacillus growth.When an acidic douche (either a self made solution with vinegar and water or a commercial preparation) is used, the pH is adjusted as is appropriate. The Massengil Company makes disposable acidic douches for your purchase over-the-counter, or you can own a douche-bag to which you will add 2-3 tablespoons of white, household vinegar and fill it with tepid water. This will give you a volume of about one quart. To douche several times a month with acidic solution is generally enough, although an increase in discharge and sexual relations, may prompt a little more need. To douche more often than once each week is usually not necessary, unless there is specific indication.

c. Act as an adjunct in the treatment of some vaginal infections.
Certain kinds of vaginal infection may prompt the need for douches
to prepare the vagina for treatment. In these situations, the character of the douche is important to consider. A neutral solution, such
as plain water, or a commercial preparation with special substances
added may be employed. In dealing with yeast or monilial infections, an alkaline douche will be necessary. A baking soda solution,
again made by the Massengil Company and found in your drugstore,
or made in your own douche bag with 3 tablespoons of baking soda
added to the quart bag of water, will work wonders. Monilia thrives
in an acid pH - to create an acid pH in the vagina with an acidic
douche only facilitates monilial growth no matter what the medicine
prescribed is intended to do. Hence, an alkaline douche not only
washes out the monilial organisms and their discharge, but it makes
the atmosphere incompatible for further yeast growth and your medicine works more effectively.

**d. Perform a cleansing activity, wash out discharge
and foreign matter.**
Those individuals who have increased discharge with rectosigmoid
vaginal construction will find douching beneficial. Those individuals
who have hair growth in the vagina because the vaginal lining has
active hair follicles in it, may at times need to douche to cleanse the
vagina of hair accumulation.

Some M-F individuals will experience vaginal dryness and commercial creams
such as Lubrin are obtainable without prescription. Others will find that vaginal
hygiene is better maintained if they use an estrogen cream periodically, insert-
ing an applicator full just after a cleansing douche. It is appropriate to do this
once a week. Placement should be at bedtime and your physician has to prescribe the vaginal estrogen cream for you. Estrogen cream so placed, does
help to maintain the vaginal lining and protects somewhat against infection.

Vaginal dilatation - We have emphasized its importance in the recovery stage
and for some months thereafter, and we have hinted at how some regularity of
sexual intercourse does away with the need for dilatation, maintaining the
caliber and length of the vagina. The human body in its self-repair and healing
tendencies always strives to come back to the original and to reestablish the
former condition. The neovaginal tunnel is not the same as a genetic female's
vagina, and without some dilatory process, either a dilator or the penetrative
penis, the neovagina may gradually shrink. Hence, for those wherein sexual
activity is absent, infrequent, or widely intermittent, some dilatation may be
necessary at times to maintain the vaginal measurements achieved at surgery
and to guard against gradual stenosis. Only the postoperative M-F can assess
that process and in your yearly gynecologic evaluations, some attention and
discussion about vaginal openness and capacity may be important to exchange

with your gynecologist. Your gynecologist should be alert to vaginal stenosis with yearly evaluations.

Self breast examinations - The incidence of serious breast disease -- malignancy for the genetic male on a hormonal regimen, appears to be no greater than for the genetic male not using a hormonal regimen. But benign breast changes can take place. Thickening, cysts and strange collections or buildup of tissue can develop and it is important to detect them and bring attention to your physician for accurate evaluation. Hence, I strongly urge you to learn the technique of self breast examination described below and to conduct it once, every month, on a specific date or day.

Admittedly, if you have had breast augmentation with saline or silicon prosthesis, the examination is more difficult. Yet in time, your awareness as to what is the usual in your own breasts becomes very accurate. The technique is not difficult, but there are no shortcuts and thoroughness is important.

.The technique is as follows - Lying down in supine position (on your back), you will examine the left breast with the right hand, the right breast with the left hand. If you are full breasted, it helps a little to place a pillow at your back with its inner margin just up to and in the length of the spine, thereby tipping you somewhat. Hence, the pillow is to the right side of your back and spine to examine the right breast, and the pillow is placed to the left side of your back and spine to examine the left breast. This keeps the breast on the front of the chest wall and tends to flatten it there. The pillow should not be overly thick. This technique allows you to feel deeply into the breast tissue even with a prosthesis beneath the breast tissue. When the breast tissue is thick or dependent (as it is when you stand or sit to examine) you can miss significant changes that are deep in the breast tissue.

Now for the right breast. Pillow in place, you will raise the right arm over your head to put the breast on a stretch, and with the fingers of the left hand extended, you feel deeply into the right breast in a rotary motion covering all quadrants of the breast, moving from the periphery to the center of the breast, the nipple area. You feel the areola and nipple region completely as well. Once you have covered all the breast in this way, then you draw the extended left hand fingers across the breast, covering it once again, in a stroking manner. This gives you two ways to evaluate the breast tissue, a) with deep point pressure and b) with a drawing or pulling of the fingers over the breast to detect any enlargements you may not have felt with the rotary pressure. Now, if anything seems different or unusual, you repeat the above maneuvers to clarify or to confirm.

Changing the pillow placement, you raise the left arm above your head and with your right hand, examine the left breast the very same way.

I stress that you lie down to examine, for when sitting in front of a mirror or standing in the shower as many women are taught to examine, your breast is compacted and dense. The breast tissue is dependent and firm, not allowing full evaluation of it as you can if it is a thinner organ with the chest wall firmly behind it. You can miss a tissue growth when it is small and in early stages, when you do not lie down to examine.

In time, you become very aware of any changes taking place in your breasts. Any change in the normal architecture becomes evident earlier with repetition and careful observation. Take the time to be thorough and be mindful of the need to always examine your breasts.

Sexual relations - These are very concerning times in the world. All too few individuals realize the dangers and difficulties with sexual experiences in this day and age. The dangers we will deal with in another section. The difficulties I refer to here, however, are in reference to comfort, performance and satisfaction. For some, there may be extended time in overcoming some of these difficulties.

To begin with, there will be a great amount of trepidation and fear when first you begin to have sex - you are really virginal in the very beginning. If the vaginal opening is tight, the caliber of the vagina a bit limited and the length a little short, you will experience discomfort and, in fact, for some -- frank pain. This will be true especially if your partner is too forceful and too anxious. You should be sure to have a tube of K-Y jelly or Surgilube, both of which are obtainable over-the-counter, and you should use it for both yourself and your partner. In time, your own lubrication may be all that is necessary. Urge your partner to be careful and gentle, and yes, even hesitant, for too much vigor and force could not only be painful, but damaging to you.

Your performance in the sexual act will be perfected with experience and time and if foreplay has been enthusiastic and complete, your sexual performance will be increasingly expert, leading to great satisfaction for you both.

Climax or orgasm is dependent on so many factors, some physical, some emotional and psychologic. If you have truly a sensate genitalia and your partner has made effort to stimulate you before penetration, then with entry you could come to adequate satisfaction or climax. Remember, you are in a very different role than you were formerly. Yet think also how rewarding and beautiful it can be for you in this capacity. You need not be altogether passive or withdrawn. Some forwardness could be a wonderful ingredient in your physical relationship. Remember also that intimacy does not always have to do with penetrative sex. Touching, caressing, holding and embracing are a few of the ways to bring pleasure and gratification to a sexual experience.

Urinary tract infections - The important point for me to emphasize for you in reference to urinary infection is this. Because of a short urethra, your protection against urinary tract infections is limited and, not as protected as when you had a considerably longer urethra. Now you are really at the same degree of risk for urinary infection as any genetic female, and for some, the risk may be greater.

Occasional urinary tract infection is not only possible, but likely, perhaps once or twice a year. Any more often, however, or any intractability in clearing a urine infection and keeping it "cured," indicates some underlying factor or set of factors to be investigated. You should then consult an urologist who can deal with this problem properly, with cultures and appropriate studies. Don't settle for repeated antibiotic trials. You want treatment based on diagnosis, not guess work!

Genital tract infections - Infection in this area can be dangerous because in these days certain genital infections can be very serious and life threatening. Fortunately, your vagina has no connection with your abdominal cavity. The genetic female does have connection through her uterus and fallopian tubes, which are open. Hence, some of the serious consequences of genital infection (pelvic inflammation, pelvic abscess, peritonitis, etc.) as they happen in the genetic female, will not develop in you. But, the neovaginal wall and vulva can still be involved in very consequential infections.
These Are:

1. Syphilis
2. Gonorrhea
3. Herpes genitalis
4. Other sexually transmitted infections, i.e. Chlamydia
5. Human immune deficiency virus (AIDS)

All of these are termed sexually transmitted diseases, and while we don't often hear any longer about syphilis and gonorrhea, these disorders are always with us and, in fact, are increasing in incidence. They are still a great problem in the world population. They are thought of by the lay individual as being focal, or limited to only the genitalia. This is not true.

Syphilis,can affect, in time, all tissues of our body, especially the cardiovascular system and the central nervous system. The primary lesion, a chancre, could be hidden in the neovagina, not obvious to you, and only hinted at by unusual vaginal discharge. It would then be confirmed in an examination by your gynecologist.

Gonorrhea, is also a disease that can attack tissues quite different from the genitalia. Gonorrhea can involve, for instance, many distant organs, even the joints of our body and its first manifestation might be only the symptoms of a urinary tract infection or an increase in vaginal discharge that has a bad aroma and some irritative qualities.

Herpes simplex genitalis is a collection of very painful ulcerations appearing in a place near to the opening of the vagina. As with all these infections, proper examination, cultures, and other forms of testing are essential to make accurate diagnosis and to institute specific therapy.

Chlamydia, or other sexually transmitted infections may only manifest themselves by an unusual vaginal discharge or a groin swelling, due to lymph node enlargement.

AIDS - The human immune deficiency virus is not so easily diagnosed at early stages. Routine testing of the blood in high risks individual may give indication of HIV positivity, but symptoms leading to a blood test that will establish HIV positivity, may develop long after viral entry into the body. While the others mentioned are serious disorders and can threaten one's health and longevity when not diagnosed early, AIDS, carries with it very, very serious consequence and death, for currently, there is no effective treatment for the disorder.

There is no real point in me giving you a detailed list of symptoms or tests and therapy for this group of diseases contracted through sexual contact. The important things to stress are these: When complaints in the urogenital tract take place, pursue them properly with your doctor and be satisfied only when his or her evaluation is complete and relieving. When you are in a relationship leading to sexual intercourse, know fully your partner's medical and sexual past. This may prove hard to do, I grant you, and it seems callous, unromantic and certainly intrusive to insist on facts before sex. Yet, many, many women are doing just that. To protect themselves, they ask for and want reassurance. Many people are not that careful or cautious and that "perfect man" coming into your life, may be bringing you some very "imperfect problems." Know also that condoms, a must **at all times**, mean **safer** sex, but not **safe** sex. They don't take the place of information about your partner's sexual habits, and infections, and recent HIV testing.

Regular medical evaluation - I have emphasized before, the need for routine and planned medical evaluation. I will do it again! And, I want to give insight into some things that should be in your mind and that of your regular physician for periodic evaluation.

1. **A gynecologic examination that includes a pap smear is essential once a year.** In the recent medical literature, there are a small number of reports of cancer involving the lining of the new vagina called squamous cell carcinoma. A pap smear of the vaginal walls can go a great distance toward making an early diagnosis of this very serious disease. All four walls of the vagina must be sampled in the pap smear.

2. **A yearly mammogram may be important** - While breast cancer is still quite uncommon in the M-F individual using hormones, there are no definitive studies in the literature and it is still unknown whether there may be a definite risk over time. Your physician's precaution and yours as well in doing this study may be all important.

3. **A periodic EKG should be done even with no cardiac history.** And it should be compared with previous studies. Once a year generally is an appropriate interval.

4. **A rectal exam and a PSA blood test should still be done once each year.** Until a definitive study proves that postoperative M-F individuals on estrogen are protected from prostatic malignancy this exam should be continued. There are a few reports in the medical literature of prostate cancer in postoperative male to female individuals implying that in some instances this disease is not male hormone dependent.

5. **Blood evaluations of liver function, lipid profile and serum prolactin studies are mandatory.** These should be conducted on a regular basis (yearly with no special problems.)

6. **Blood studies for AIDS and hepatitis should be a part of the yearly evaluation**. These should be especially conducted for individuals thought to be particularly at risk.

Special thoughts for the Male to Female individual to know - M-F

Genetic women in all of their lives have experienced things you will never know and, in fact, may not be aware. There will be times when you may be drawn into conversations that deal with situations and topics that you should have information about even with no prior experience. Women discuss these experiences with each other. They talk about menses and pregnancy and sex. At work, at a social event, in a variety of places and times, you may be quite outstanding if you have no contribution to make to those conversations. Let's alter that with some basic information:

Menses and menopause - Menstrual flow begins for a few young girls as early as 9 years of age, for others, as late as 16 or 17 years of age. The average is 12-14 years and it is preceded by pubertal change, that is, breast development, changes in skin texture, hair growth and other developments, for example accentuation of hips, waist and derriere and growth of pubic (genital) and axillary (armpit) hair. Other hormones are activated as well, in particular, growth hormone. Hence, changes in stature and development of the chest cage and pelvic bones. Menses last 5-7 days in these individuals and are very often heavy and painful with a great deal of debility for several days of the period. This may last for one to several years. In time, for most, the periods assume a very regular pattern, usually 27-32 days apart and become much less difficult. Cramps are easily relieved and the flow is less vigorous. Some, however, in their teens continue to have greatly disturbing pain and it is felt by researchers that about 1/3 of these young women with such severe pain associated with periods (called dysmenorrhea) will prove later in life to have a disorder known as endometriosis. In later life, some of these individuals with endometriosis are infertile to a lesser or greater degree. Most with endometriosis will continue to have heavy flow and continued pain problems throughout their entire reproductive life.

For most individuals, menses become routine. They are often an annoyance and an interruption to daily activities and plans. A few look at menses as a real affirmation of their femaleness and "to not have periods is not to be female." This of course is not true, but it is the emblem or badge some women believe to be confirmatory. Pregnancy may interrupt the menstrual pattern a number of times, but as life goes on, several things begin to develop. We will devote more time to premenstrual syndrome, but it now becomes more evident as the genetic female gets older. That "period before the period" is one of very uncomfortable physical and psychologic change, and some really have problems for 5-10 days before menstrual flow begins.

In time, at an average of 45 years, but for some at a younger and quite a few an older age, menses will change notably in timing, in character and in volume. Some months, there is no menstrual period. In some months, there are two periods and in addition, the onset of hot flashes and changes in libido (an indifference to sexual relations) and physical changes, such as weight gain due to calories and fluid retention, are a part of the annoying and often devastating picture.

Headaches are severe and long-lasting and hard to relieve. Chest palpitations and sweating are frequent complaints.

A host of psychologic patterns develop as well for some. The feelings of approaching older age, the loss of attractiveness, particularly to a husband or lover, the loss of ability to conceive (which is such a confirmation of youth and beauty for some,) the loss of family, with children leaving home -- a host of emotionally trying mental states take place. Health states and financial concerns, marital strife and many other factors add considerably to the stress and discomfort of being menopausal.

Pregnancy - Once a genetic female becomes ovulatory (that is, she produces an egg in mid-menstrual cycle,) she is capable of conceiving a pregnancy. She will continue to be capable of conception if she maintains a normal and healthful gynecologic health status up to that time when she becomes perimenopausal. When she becomes irregular in her ovulation along with other factors in her gynecologic health, her ability to conceive and/or to take a pregnancy to term (forty weeks,) are limited. Women in years past had big families. It wasn't unusual to know families with 5-8 or more children. Now women generally have no more than two and they conceive later in their fertile years. Often the first pregnancy begins after the age of 30.

Many sociologic factors account for this. The pursuit of career, need for income for a variety of reasons, reluctance to have large families because of expense, and the long time in rearing and educating children -- these are just some of the many reasons.

Women now plan their pregnancies using various birth control methods to assist them. In addition, some women seem to be very oriented towards two very important considerations:

1. If this is not a time for pregnancy, then abortion is an alternative.

2. Science has developed ways to determine the health and sex of the pregnancy at a very early stage in the pregnancy. Once again, abortion is an alternative if the pregnancy is not perfect or wanted.

Perhaps this is a time for us to look at abortion as well since it is common in occurrence and can have such impact on the individuals life and future.

Abortions can be spontaneous, by that I mean they happen without planning and interference (this occurs in about 10% of all pregnancies) or they may be therapeutic, which means intended or instrumental interruption. For those experiencing a spontaneous abortion, this is always a devastating experience, no matter what the cause. There are a number of medical reasons why this takes place. The first thing to know is that nothing the mother does or doesn't do is responsible for the pregnancy loss (which usually occurs in the first trimester or first three months.) She has no control over the events as they unfold. In fact, one reassuring point to make is that over 50%, perhaps even 60% of all spontaneous abortions take place because of a genetic defect - the pregnancy is not normal and shouldn't continue to term. Of the remaining 40% of spontaneous abortions, a very high number are **not** going to be repeated in a subsequent pregnancy and if repeated, reasons for repetition are diagnosable and treatable. For each and every woman experiencing a spontaneous abortion, the experience is tragic, filled with loss and grief. It is believed that this is failure. She has guilt and believes she will never be pregnant again. It is a time for much support and need for reassurance by those around this woman. It is a time when the genetic female feels very lost and depressed.

Therapeutic abortions, while they are planned and determined, are still very emotional experiences. There is often guilt and hesitancy before it is carried out and often grief and self recrimination after it is over. It is a very difficult decision and some few do not get over the interruption. It reaches far out into their lives, even after one or several pregnancies take place and go to term successfully.

Once an individual is pregnant, their joy is great and expectation, and great planning and readiness are evident. The pregnant woman is fulfilled. The various tests and involvements with diet, exercise, instruction and preparation for labor and delivery with plan for a natural childbirth, a sharing with husband and family, all of this is very beautiful and special. No matter what the problems or discomforts that take place, there is generally a very wonderful and mystified feeling that accompanies these difficulties. The obstetrician and his or her staff are very important people in her life and her dedication and energy to have all come to a perfect conclusion may exclude at time the baby's father, work responsibilities and other people and events that have some claim on her. It is a challenging but gratifying psychologic experience for that woman.

Labor is anticipated and desired, yet denied and unwanted when it happens -- all of these at the same time. It can be easy and short. It can be lengthy and overwhelming. It can be very painful and frustrating and the ultimate frustration has to be when a Caesarian section must be done. Some fear this, for it is major surgery and filled with unknowns. "Will the baby be all right? - Will I be all right?" A Caesarian section can be an emergency and that is very concerning to the mother and all around her. It can be a great disappointment to her plans and, in fact, it may represent an insult and intrusion on her person and on her ability to do it all in a "natural way." She may have great relief that a section was done, yet she may demonstrate great anger that it was done. These emotions may have a hold on her for long years to come.

The premenstrual syndrome - For some genetic females, this unpleasant time begins at mid-cycle, just after ovulation, building up in intensity as one approaches the onset of menstrual flow. For others this terrible experience may last a short time, involving only three or four days before the period begins. The discomforts of this time are multiple and have to do with changes in hormonal ratios in the blood and the utilization of progesterone, in particular, by the tissues or end organs that use it. Once the period begins, the symptoms disappear.

Women experience a variety of symptoms in varying degrees. Fluid retention, weight increase, and breast discomfort are frequent complaints. The unrelenting desire to eat certain foods is a real problem for some because their discomforts are made worse by these things, for example chocolate and salt. The real burden for some women is the marked personality changes they experience. They are aware that it is happening, but they have no control over these wide mood swings. They lash out at all around them - children, husbands, friends, fellow employees. The misery of it for some, forces the use of medication and diet restrictions when they bring the problem to their doctors.

Communicative skills and ability to relate to others - M-F

Genetic females have a built-in capacity to relate easily and to connect effectively with others. They exercise the ability to negotiate and to neutralize, frequently every day as they move through various social situations. Genetic men in contrast, use a very dominant aggressive approach to those around them. To achieve, to be on top of, to dominate -- all of these, is a predominant trait and a way of life for males. A mix of these traits, to know when to negotiate and then when to be demanding is the ideal. This androgyny in one's personality is what you really want to achieve. The real message I want to give to you is this. You have made your physical appearance as female as possible. Your body now has conformity with your gender identity (that perception of yourself.) You may have worked very successfully to alter your voice. Your gestures and body language may be perfect for the new you and your taste in fashions may be impeccable. If you still present yourself with the typical masculine attitude and thought process, you will fail in virtually all of your social endeavors. You should have been developing that mystical, feminine approach to all around you in the years that it has taken for you to come to this point in your life. However, it is not too late. You need only to be aware that change may be necessary and then take the steps to make that change.

I have observed a great number of M-F transsexuals. Some have that true female attitude deep within them, and I think it's really a part of their gender identity from very early years. Others have grasped the idea and are successful in making change and becoming "the woman." Many stay strongly male and are not fully aware that they are dominant and overpowering. Don't be one of the last group. Lucky you will be if you are one of the first group, but should you be with those in the second group, congratulations to you for your awareness and for your adaptability. You may have to continue working on it for a time, but it will soon become a coat, easily worn.

Specific thoughts for Female to Male individuals in daily living F-M

The new male seems to make a wonderful adaptation to his new existence. Adjustments to family, loved ones, friends and the workplace seem to be far easier and much more firmly established than is often the case for the M-F individual. I congratulate you, for while the transition and surgery is very difficult from many standpoints, you almost invariably come through it to this time in your life with strength and maturity. You "fit in" and blend so successfully. It's wonderful to observe.

I want to emphasize to you the importance in maintaining your physical health as strongly as you have before this. There are a few things I want to call to your attention.

Continue your hormonal therapy - It may be with evaluation and discussion with your physician that you can begin to use a lower dose and perhaps a different way of administration. That will be an issue that is specific to you in your medical care. It may be that in a very short time a good transdermal approach will be available and you can use a skin patch to continue your testosterone regimen. To get rid of those needles would be a blessing! But, you need the testosterone to help with bone metabolism. This hormone does play a part in keeping your skeletal system sound, strong and healthy. Don't stop it unless some medical condition warrants its interruption.

Other medications as they are needed to maintain your health must be used as they are prescribed by your physician. Don't deny their importance. I suggest the use of one adult aspirin tablet each day to influence the coagulation system in the blood stream. This lowers the risk of clot formation in the veins (thrombophlebitis) and blockade of the arteries, particularly those of the heart and the brain. Some individuals feel that vitamins in sensible doses are important when taken daily. I don't object to this, though I do believe that with good balance in one's diet and proper planning in food preparation, you will ingest adequate vitamins in your food.

The question of infection - Infections in some degree will always be with us. A yearly cold, or chronic sinus infections are poignant examples of this, but special areas where infection is apt to set up "housekeeping." include:

     a. The urinary tract
     b. The genital tract

The urinary tract - In theory, you should be protected from bladder and upper urinary tract infection by the lengthened urethra you now possess. However, conditions prior to this may have influenced the urinary tract for a tendency to repeated and frequent infection. If bladder infections were a problem before surgery, and a surgical influence is added to that chronic problem, then likely you will be burdened with this great concern now and for some time to come. If the various procedures and manipulations associated with surgery gave to you a tendency for recurrent infection, this may not disappear altogether once the surgical care is completed. Hopefully, none of these factors will exist and your urinary tract will be healthy and totally functional. Any hint of infection, a burning sensation with voiding, feelings of frequency and/or urgency to void must be reported to your doctor, and I would urge that the physician obtain urine cultures to identify the bacterial organism quickly and give therapy as specifically as possible. Repeated infection in this system must be investigated with the testing indicated, and even cystoscopy (a look inside the bladder with a special instrument) may be called for. Lower tract infections (the urethra and the bladder) can lead to upper tract infection (the kidneys) and that is a very serious consequence.

Previously we spoke of the development of fistulas in the urinary tract, particularly where the segments of the neourethra are joined together. This is a very annoying, compromising problem, but it usually manifests itself in the early convalescence, or early in the late convalescence. The likelihood of one developing in later life, is very uncommon. Evidence of poor urinary tract function, i.e. incontinence, dribbling, signs of retained or residual urine, interrupted urinary stream passage -- all of these must be reported to a urologist who has cared for you before, or to whom your medical physician now refers you.

The genital tract - In the phalloplasty procedure, some surgeons modify or obliterate the vagina. Others will leave it intact and place the phallus over it. You must know quite accurately just what was done, because an intact vagina will perhaps have discharge and potentially could be involved in various infections, in particular, Monilia. Monilial infection can begin just with taking an antibiotic for another problem. In addition, while likely remote, other bacterial infections could develop. Also, if it should be that you never had the uterus removed, there is still potential, though remote, for malignant change in the cervix or the lining of the uterus (endometrium.) The vaginal walls and the cervix need pap smear evaluations periodically, even after phalloplasty. When we consider the phallus as the site of infection, much more concerning possibilities exist.

> a. Syphilis
> b. Gonorrhea
> c. Herpes genitalis
> d. Non-gonorrheal urethritis (Chlamydia)
> e. Human immune deficiency virus infection (AIDS)

These are known as sexually transmitted diseases. And, while we don't often hear any longer about syphilis and gonorrhea, these disorders are always with us and are, in fact, increasing in incidence. They are thought of by the lay individual as being focal or limited only to the genitalia. This is not true.

Syphilis - can affect in time all tissues of our body, especially the cardiovascular and central nervous systems. The primary lesion, the chancre, could be hidden in the folds of the scrotum or may even be found on the penile shaft. You will observe it as a very firm and growing ulceration, and it must be reported immediately to your doctor.

Gonorrhea - is also a disease that can attack tissues quite different from the genitalia. In uncommon, but very definite instances, our joints can be diseased by the gonorrheal bacterial organism.

Herpes simplex genitalis - is a collection of very painful ulcerations appearing on the penis or over the newly created scrotum. It can be very debilitating and uncomfortable. With this infection, as with all infections, proper examination, inclusive of cultures and other forms of testing is essential to make sure accurate diagnosis and specific therapy is instituted.

Non-Gonorrheal urethritis - is caused by the Chlamydial bacterial organism. This will be responsible for painful urination and frequency, and can sometimes be associated with an unusual discharge coming from the tip of the phallus. It needs prompt identification and very specific antibiotic therapy.

AIDS - The immune deficiency virus is not so easily diagnosed at early stages. Routine testing of the blood in high risk individuals may give indication of HIV positivity, but symptoms leading to a blood test that will establish HIV positivity may develop long after viral entry into the body. While the others mentioned are serious disorders and can threaten one's health and longevity, AIDS, carries with it very, very serious consequences and death.

There is no point in me giving you detailed lists of symptoms and tests and therapy for this group of diseases contracted through sexual contact. The important things to stress are these: When complaints in the urogenital tract take place, pursue them properly with your doctor and be satisfied only when his or her evaluation is complete and relieving. When you are in a relationship leading to sexual intercourse, know fully your partner's medical and sexual past. This may be hard to do, I grant you, and it seems callous and unromantic and certainly intrusive to insist on facts before fooling around. Yet, in this day and age, many individuals are doing just that. To protect themselves, they ask questions and want reassurance. To inquire about previous sexual infections and the date of the last HIV testing is really a good idea. Many sexual partners are not that careful or cautious and that perfect individual coming into your life, may bring to you some very imperfect problems.

With effective and appropriate stiffening devices, penetration can be very complete and satisfying, but to avoid contracting the above disorders, I advise that you always use a condom. It will help to insure **safer** sex, though it's not a guarantee for all times, in all ways.

The value and importance of regular medical care can't be stressed enough- It makes good sense to see a medical physician at least once each year for a routine physical exam and appropriate blood studies, along with special testing. We have mentioned in previous sections some of the concerns that are associated with taking a testosterone medication. Those studies that are particularly necessary for you to have, are related to those concerns.

If not indicated more often, an electrocardiogram study once each year is certainly warranted as part of your evaluation. Along with it, cardiac stress studies that are important or indicated should be done as well. Comparison with past studies is highly necessary. A rectal exam is very important, because this exam can be very helpful in diagnosing malignant disease of the lower rectum in a significant number of individuals, early, when the developing cancer is within reach of the examining finger. In blood evaluations, while other studies are important as well, the liver enzymes, lipid profile and a complete blood cell analysis and count are necessary. Testing for AIDS and hepatitis virus may be very important, particularly for those who are at increased risk.

Special thoughts for the Female to Male to know - F-M

I don't have a great deal more to share with you, but I would emphasize the great need for you to be conscious of your physical health, to be watchful of your diet and weight, and that you exercise regularly and comfortably. Over-weight leads to some very compromising medical disorders, i.e. hypertension, and for those who are susceptible to it, diabetes, and subsequently, heart and vessel disease. I don't believe you should be ritualistic or make health the dominant, all encompassing feature of your life, but to keep it in perspective and to moderate in all things to insure comfort and continued good health, is to your advantage.

Lastly, there is no doubt that the masculine approach to life is what you want. The aggressive, dominant attitude, the one- upmanship, all of this is important. It compliments your new body and appearance. Yet, I urge you to retain some of the ability to connect and some of the ability to negotiate. These features are so characteristic of the genetic female. To have a generous mix of the male and female is the ideal. You are much more balanced and mature. To know when to demand, when to use tact, when to use a diplomatic approach to someone or some circumstance is a gift. You were born with it, and while you may have suppressed it for a long time, now make the effort to bring it back into your life. To be demanding and overpowering can be a burden for others in your life, and in time, it will prove to be so for you. Your hormones lend some of this attitude to you. It may have become more evident as you began to use them, and as you continue their use, but your mind can guide you to travel a middle ground. Life will be sweeter and more fruitful.

PART 2

Legal Issues

MARTINE ALIANA ROTHBLATT, J.D.

*"Ultimately, it is the law that
declares us Male or Female."*

E - THE LAW AND THE TRANSSEXUAL DURING TRANSITION M-F/F-M

The need to follow certain pathways to correct and appropriate documentation is very real. Too often the transgendered individual doesn't know the process and experiences many frustrations and delays in the preparation for a new and legal identity. This section gives a very orderly and expert approach to all that is needed and will help to make all work as it should.

Ultimately, the sex that you are is as much a legal determination as it is a medical *fait accomplis*. To many, this seems surprising. After all, what does a judge in a black robe have to do with my genitals? Well, in the United States, the judge in a black robe won't have much to do with your genitals, but he or she will have a lot do with your sex. This was learned first hand by the famous ophthalmologist and tennis star, Dr. Renee Richards.

In 1975, at the age of 41, Renee Richards underwent male-to-female sex reassignment surgery. Prior to that date she had played tennis as a man, winning often in men's professional competition. After her surgery, she competed as a woman in nine women's tennis tournaments, winning twice and finishing as a runner-up three times. In 1977 she sought to participate in the Women's Division of the United States Tennis Association (USTA) national championships in Forest Hills, New York. She was told that she could not compete as a woman unless she passed a sex chromosome test, known as the "Barr body" test, to prove she was female. Dr. Richards found that despite her years of taking female hormones, her psychologically female orientation, and her sex reassignment surgery, it was going to take a judge to decide that she was a woman and could thus compete in women's professional tennis. Hence she filed suit for a declaratory judgement against the USTA.

Both the defendants, USTA, and the plaintiff, Dr. Richards, retained law firms and presented expert witnesses to Judge Alfred M. Ascione of the New York Supreme Court. The defendant's expert claimed:

> *Sexual identity is a complex pattern of which some features are immutable (the nuclear and chromosomal); some can be effaced but not converted to their opposite (the gonadal and ductal structures); some are alterable by surgery or drugs (the external genitalia and hormonal balance); and some are largely subjective (the psychological and social sex).*

The defendant's expert would not claim that Dr. Richards was either male or female, only that if she failed to pass a chromosome test that reveals the presence of a second X chromosome (the "Barr body" test), then she was probably not a woman. If fact, Dr. Richards had twice taken the Barr body test as the

USTA demanded, but the hospital laboratory reported ambiguous results due to their failure to follow proper test procedures! USTA demanded a third test, which Dr. Richards refused to take.

Dr. Richards presented several expert witnesses in her behalf. One witness, Dr. Leo Wollman, had probably treated more transsexuals than anyone else at the time -- over 1,700. He testified that:

> *Dr. Richards should be considered female. The Barr test would classify Dr. Richards as a male and despite the fact that the chromosomes may appear to be that of a man, if she has the external genital appearance, the internal organ appearance, gonadal identity, endocrinological makeup and psychological and social development of a female, she would be considered a female by any reasonable test of sexuality.*

Dr. Richard's gynecologist testified that she "examines as woman." But perhaps the most powerful testimony for Dr. Richards came from the famous sexologist, Dr. John Money. He observed that the Barr body test is inadequate for determining sex, and would occasionally produce inaccurate results, because there are many people who do not belong to the typical statistical chromosome pattern (e.g. Kleinfelter's and Turner's syndromes, among others.) Dr. Money concluded:

> *The Barr test would work an injustice since by all other known indicators of sex, Dr. Richards is a female, e.g., external genital appearance is that of a female, her internal sex is that of a female who has been hysterectomized and ovariectomized; Dr. Richards is psychologically a woman; endocrinological female; somatically (muscular tone, height, weight, breast, physique) Dr. Richards is female and muscular and fat composition has been transformed to that of a female; socially Dr. Richards is female; Dr. Richards' gonadal status is that of an ovariectomized female.*

Judge Ascione gave great weight to Dr. Money's testimony. He noted that Dr. Money felt that a "person such as Dr. Renee Richards should be classified as female and for anyone in the medical or legal field to find otherwise is completely unjustified." Hence the judge concluded that when a person finds it necessary to undergo a sex reassignment, "the unfounded fears and misconceptions of defendants must give way to the overwhelming medical evidence that this person is now female."

The USTA was ordered to permit Dr. Richards to compete in the tournament. She finished as a doubles finalist, went on to coach Martina Navratilova through her 1982 Wimbledon win, and then returned to her ophthalmology practice.[5]

The lesson of the Renee Richards case is that the law is very important to any transsexual. Ultimately it is the law, based upon medical evidence, which declares us either male or female. The reason for this is that "male" and "female" are really social labels. In the "real world" we are just people with biology. We can demand that people treat us as our chosen sexual identity, but people can also refuse to accede to our demands. When they refuse, we have but four choices:

1. Ignore their refusal;
2. Continue to persuade them;
3. Use illegal means to force them to accept us;
4. Get a judge to order them to accept us.

Had Renee Richards taken track (1) or (2) above, she would not have been able to play tennis professionally. Similarly, if we limit ourselves to only tracks (1) and (2) in our lives, then we may lose out on many opportunities that we want to pursue. Had Renee Richards taken track (3) above, she would probably have been arrested. Similarly, if we use violence, intimidation or other illegal means of getting people to accept our sexual identity, then we may end up in jail. But if we get the law on our side, then someone who messes with us is messing with the judge. Ultimately, that means contempt of court and time in jail -- for our detractors.

Whether chromosomes, behavior, genitals or birth certificates are needed to force someone to accept our sexual identity is a decision, in the final analysis, which can only be made by a court of law. Hence this chapter will now focus on putting together the legal pieces of paper needed to buttress our chosen sexual identity.

Change of Name

During the transition period, it is generally possible to convert every piece of one's identification to the chosen sexual identity except for the birth certificate. We say "generally possible" because, except for passports, there is no national identification policy in the United States -- each state and city is free to follow their own rules on personal identification. Usually, they have vague rules regarding change of name and no rules regarding change of sex. Thus, one is at the mercy of the discretion of various bureaucrats and local judges. It is because of this discretion factor that we say it is "generally possible" to change the sex and name on all your identification during transition. It is generally *possible*, because it has been done thousands of times, and we will tell you how to most likely succeed. But there will be exceptions, and we will provide advice later on how to deal with those exceptions.

There are two basic ways to change one's name and sexual identity in the United States. We'll describe both, but we recommend you use the second method for fewer hassles. Nevertheless, the first method is less expensive initially, and can always be used even if the second method fails.

The first method for change of identity is by "Common Usage." The United States recognize the basic right of a person to change their name and gender identity. Americans are very lucky in this regard, because in continental Europe, and everywhere else that the Napoleonic legal code prevails, there is no basic right to change one's identity. Under the Napoleonic code there is the concept of "inalienable birth status," which makes it difficult to change one's name except for compelling reasons. But in the United States, you can change your name for any reason whatsoever so long as there is no intention to defraud others.

Under the Common Usage method of identity change, one acquires a legal right to be recognized by a new name and gender identity simply by the sole and consistent use of that new identity. For example, if starting today, a person previously known as Ms. Jane Summer told everyone who know her/him that his new name was Mr. Jack Frost, after about one year Jack would have acquired a legal right to his new name and gender identity so long as (1) Jack consistently used only his new name, and (2) Jack did not try to defraud anybody.

Practically speaking, it is often difficult to get people to simply start calling you a new name. Companies that you deal with may often respond that they want something "official" before they address you in the new name. You can get around this problem for less than $100 by having a lawyer write the following type of letter for you on his or her stationery:

This Common Usage method of identity change is legally valid. One may obtain most any type of identification with this method. The problems with it are (1) it can be lengthy, since companies or agencies may demand that you have spent at least a year under Common Usage before they recognize it, and (2) it can require additional letters from your lawyer explaining to reluctant companies or agencies that the Common Usage method is just as legal as a judge's order. Hence, the Common Usage method may end up being fairly expensive in the long run.

SAMPLE COMMON USAGE LAWYER'S LETTER

May B. Judicious, Esq.
Attorney at Law
123 Main Street
Anywhere, USA 01234
Phone: 555-654-3210

Date

Concerned Party's Address
123 Main Street
Anywhere, USA 55555

To whom it may concern:

Please be advised that we represent Mr. Jack Frost, formerly Ms. Jane Summer, in the manner of his/her change of name.

Mr. Frost is changing his name and gender identity under the common law method of Common Usage.

He will be consistently and exclusively referred to as Mr. Jack Frost henceforth. Mr. Jack Frost is responsible for any obligations incurred heretofore in the name of Ms. Jane Summer.
Henceforth, please direct all documentation and invoices to him as Mr. Jack Frost.

(Signature)
May B. Judicious, Esq.

MBJ/prp

The second method to changing one's identity is with a Judge's Order. All states have a specific law section that specifies the conditions for a change of name. Common to all states, however, is that a judge will change a name for any reason, including transsexualism, so long as no fraud is involved. So there would generally be no problem with getting a Judge to change the name Ms. Jane Summer to Mr. Jack Frost. Remember, however, that since judges have discretion, it is always possible that you will get the sexist judge that won't change your name without proof that you are a transsexual. In that case, you'll need to simply get a letter from your psychiatrist.

It is possible to change one's own name under the Judge's Order method without using a lawyer. A lawyer might charge several hundred dollars. To do it yourself, you will generally need to do at least the following:

- Prepare a Petition for Name Change;
- Comply with a local publication requirement;
- Prepare a Judge's Final Decree;
- Pay the Court's Filing Fees, and perhaps show up in court.

A sample of the court documents that are needed to prepare for Jane Summer transitioning to Jack Frost are provided on the following pages. Just make the appropriate name and gender transpositions for a male-to-female transition.

Please remember that each state has slightly different rules, especially with regard to publishing your petition in a local newspaper (usually in the "legal notices" section.) You need to ask the court clerk what these rules are.

Even if you make mistakes, however, the clerk at the court will probably tell you what to change in your write-up to get the court to accept it. The whole process should not take more than three months.

SAMPLE PETITION FOR NAME CHANGE

In The [Name of Local Court] for
[Name of Local Community], [State]

In the Matter of   )
The Petition of   )
Ms. Jane Summer, aka,   )
                                              Civil Number: [Leave for Clerk]
J. Summer   )
)
                                              PETITION FOR A CHANGE OF NAME
for a Change of Name to   )
)
Mr. Jack Frost   )
)
Date of Birth: Your Birthdate
Social Security Number: Your SS Number
Address: Your Address
Phone: Your Phone

J. Summer, Petitioner and Affiant, respectfully represents to the
Court as follows:

1. That petitioner is of full age and has been a resident of [Your
locality, and state] for over [number] of years.

2. That petitioner's present full and correct name is Ms. Jane
Summer.

3. That petitioner respectfully request that this court grant a
change of name to Mr. Jack Frost.

4. That petitioner desires this change of name because he is
transsexual and has been living and working as a man since
[date], at which time he commenced hormonal sex reassignment therapy; that he has and is using the name Jack Frost
both in his business and in his social relations; that the change
of name requested herein will promote petitioner's peace of
mind, is in keeping with petitioner's personal taste and changes
the legal name to the name commonly used by petitioner.

5. That petitioner further request an Order changing the gender designation on petitioner's driver's license in order to conform the gender designation to his new legal name and to his appearance. The change of gender designation from F to M will allow petitioner to conduct certain business such as cashing checks, setting up bank accounts etc.; will not be detrimental to any person or to the state of [name of state]; and will assist the state in the event the state needs to find and locate petitioner because the gender designation will be consistent with petitioner's name and appearance.

6. That the change of name is proper and is not being done for any illegal, fraudulent, obscene or otherwise offensive purpose, and does not interfere with the rights of others. No creditor and no other person will be damaged by the change of name and gender identity.

7. Upon receipt of the Order changing the name, petitioner will notify any and all concerned creditors, banks, government agencies and all interested persons of said Order.

8. It is petitioner's intention to use the name **Mr. Jack Frost** consistently and non-fraudulently.

WHEREFORE, petitioner prays for an Order changing the name of Ms. Jane Summer to Mr. Jack Frost, for an Order changing the gender designation on petitioner's driver's license from F to M and for such further Orders as may be proper.

I DO SOLEMNLY DECLARE AND AFFIRM UNDER THE PENALTIES OF PERJURY THAT THE CONTENTS OF THE FOREGOING PETITION ARE TRUE AND CORRECT.

_____

J. Summer, Petitioner and Affiant

_____

Notary

SAMPLE FINAL DECREE

In The [Name of Local Court] for [Name of Local Community], [State]

In the Matter of	)	
The Petition of	)	
Ms. Jane Summer		
, aka, J. Summer	)	Civil Number:
		[Get from Clerk]
	)	PETITION FOR A CHANGE
for a Change of Name to	)	OF NAME
	)	
Mr. Jack Frost	)	

Final Decree

Upon consideration of the Petition filed by J. Summer and Notice by Publication in the [Name of Newspaper] having occurred for [number of weeks required in your locale], and it appearing that there are good and sufficient grounds for granting the relief sought, it is this ____[Leave blank for judge]_____ day of ____[Leave blank for judge] _____, by the [Name of Court, Locality, State],

ADJUDGED, ORDERED AND DECREED, that the name of Ms. Jane Summer is changed to Mr. Jack Frost, and that the gender designation on petitioner's driver's license be changed from F to M.

_____
JUDGE

You must file both the petition for the name change and the final decree, properly filled out, and with the Court's filing fee, to get the name change process started. The reason for the Final Decree is so that all that the Judge needs to do to give you what you want is to fill in the date and sign his or her name. Remember, you must also find out what the local newspaper publication requirement is, comply with it, and file back with the Court proof that you complied (such as clippings stapled to a page with your caption, name and file number on it.)

Often times you will get the Final Decree you want in the mail and will never even have to show up in Court. If you show up, make sure you look your gender best. It is possible that the judge might ask for proof that you are a transsexual. In this case, a letter from your psychiatrist will suffice.

It is also possible that the judge might give you the name change, but not the gender change on your driver's license until you have a sex change operation. If that occurs, it is best to get a lawyer to ask the judge to reconsider, arguing that the purpose of the driver's license is best served by having the sex on the license conform to what you actually look like. If you are still unsuccessful, you can always move to another county or township and try again in a different court. Alternatively, you could ask a lawyer to appeal the judges's decision to a higher judge. No one gender-change method will work 100% of the time because judges have a lot of discretion over what to do. However, the method recommended herein will work for most people throughout the United States.

Change of Documentation

Once your name and gender identity have been changed as previously described, it is next necessary to communicate that change with the issuers of the various licenses, cards and records that you may hold. The more typical sorts of documentation requiring notification of gender change are as follows:

Social Security Card

The Social Security Administration (SSA) has a one page form for change of name. Get this name change from your local SSA office and fill it out. On the box which says "sex" check your new sexual identification. You should also include the legal documentation you are using for change of identity. The SSA will readily accept the Judge's Order method, but eventually they could be made to accept the Common Usage method.

In the event a SSA bureaucrat sends you a form letter that they have changed your name but not your sex, it will be necessary to send them a psychologist's letter to the effect that you are a transsexual that has transitioned from the old sex to the new sex. It they write back and say that they require a birth certificate in the new sex, then you are probably out of luck and must wait until you have your sex reassignment surgery. Alternatively, they simply may ask for proof of the new sex. If you are male-to-female, one alternative may be to send the SSA a letter from a cooperative doctor that says you are a woman with clitoral hypertrophy, vaginal agenesis and ectopic ovaries. (The alternative for a female-to-male would be a man with penile hypotrophy and scrotal agenesis.) This keeps the doctor honest (there is no single agreed medical definition of what is a woman and what is a man) and gives the SSA bureaucrat the piece of proof that they may need saying you are of a new sex.

Professional Licensure

It is relatively easy to obtain professional licensure in your new name and gender. However, professional licensing agencies will want to see a Judge's Order rather than an attorney's Common Usage letter. Simply send a letter to your professional association in charge of licensing stating that you have changed your sex and name and to please re-issue your license in your new name and gender. Most professional licenses don't reflect gender, so they will probably ignore that part. Make sure to include the Judge's Order.

Driving License

Previously, we discussed the best way to obtain a new driver's license. With a Judge's Order to change name and sex, the motor vehicle department has no choice but to comply. However, if the judge strikes out the part of the Final Decree dealing with gender, and simply changes your name, there are other alternatives available to you. The simplest is to obtain a standard letter from a gender services psychologist that reads more or less as follows:

SAMPLE PSYCHOLOGIST'S LETTER

Dr. R.U. Nutts
Licensed Psychologist
123 Main Street
Anywhere, USA 12345

Date

To whom it may concern:

This is to certify that [new name] is a preoperative transsexual. [She/He] is at present time undergoing psychological therapy in preparation for [his/her] transsexual surgery. Treatment requires living full time as a [woman/man] prior to surgery. Therefore, [she/he] should be afforded all the rights of a [female/male] and be considered and treated as a [female/male] in every respect. This includes documents such as driver's license and passport.

[Signature]
R.U. Nutts, Ph.D.
[State] License # PS-444555

Such a letter, together with either the Common Usage or Judge's Order method of name change should suffice for the driver's license agency to change both your name and sex designation on your license. Make sure to look your gender best when you arrive for your picture to be taken, because the desk clerk who processes your application will also probably have his or her supervisor come out to take a look at you.

In the worst case, the local driver's license agency will be willing to change your name but not your sex. In this case, you have three choices:

1) Go ahead and get your new license with the name and photo change alone. Rarely will anyone look close enough at your license to see what sex it says. Most people, for purposes such as check cashing, will just look at the picture which should match your new gender identity and name. If police stop you and raise a sexual identity questions, just pull out your handy psychologist's letter.

2) Wait until after your sex reassignment surgery, when a new birth certificate is possible. Then without any doubt you can get the sex box changed on the license.

3) Go to a different branch of the motor vehicle agency. You may have just run across a sexist bureaucrat and you may have better luck elsewhere. There is nothing illegal with doing this.

Credit Cards and Household Bills

Credit cards and household bills are very easy to change. A simple letter from you to change your name and gender identity will almost always suffice. To be on the safe side, and save a second round of postage stamps, you can include a copy of your Judge's Order or lawyer's Common Usage letter.

It is very important to change all of your credit cards and household bills to your new name. One of the key criteria for upholding your right to your new name against any possible challenges later on is that you have used your new name exclusively and consistently.

School Records

School records will ordinarily be modified based simply on a letter to the registrar, with a Judge's Order or attorney's Common Usage letter enclosed. It is often helpful to have a lawyer draft the letter on his or stationery to give it a more "official" bearing. A form letter which has worked well in the past is provided on the next page.

SAMPLE SCHOOL RECORDS
CHANGE OF NAME/SEX LETTER

May B. Judicious, Esq.
Attorney At Law
123 Main Street
Anywhere, USA 01234
Phone (123) 555-7890

Date

Ivory Tower University
31416 Einstein Road
Relativity, USA 13571-1131

Re: Request of update records of Jack Frost ne
     Jane Summer Social Security Number: 123-45-6789

Dear Registrar:

My client Jack Frost wishes to have all of his Ivory Tower records
updated to reflect his name change and sex status. Please find
enclosed a copy of the court order effecting his change in name.
He was a student at Ivory Tower from [dates] and received his
[degree] in [date], a copy of which is enclosed.

If it appears in your records and transcripts, please be sure to
also update his sex status from F to M. My client is willing to pay
any required fees, and he requests that an official transcript be
sent directly to him verifying that his records have been correctly updated.

If possible, he requests that a corrected Graduate Certificate be
issued in his new name, for which he will cover the costs. Given
his unique circumstances, your sensitivity in meeting his request will be most gratefully appreciated. Please send all related correspondence directly to my client at [address]. You can
contact my client directly with any questions at [phone num-
ber].

Sincerely,
[signature]
May B. Judicious

Banks

Bank records can ordinarily be changed as readily as credit cards, except bank officers are more likely to insist on seeing a Judge's Order instead of a lawyer's Common Usage letter. However, if you have already obtained your new driver's license, a bank will undoubtedly accept that in connection with a Common Usage letter. Make sure to re-sign your signature cards with the new name. Also be sure to have your name changed on safety deposit box contracts and on any accounts for which you are a beneficiary or trustee.

Passport

The policy of the passport office fluctuates a bit with regard to transsexuals, and not all of the field offices follow or know what the Passport Office's overall policy is from time-to-time. Generally speaking, you have an excellent chance of getting a passport issued in your new name and sexual identity if you fill out a new passport form, put in the appropriate information, and include both a judge's Final Decree and a psychologist's letter, as described above.

Sometimes, the new passport will be issued to you for only short duration, such as until such time as the Passport Office believe you will have had your sexual reassignment surgery. The Passport Office may ask you or your psychologist for that information, or they may simply issue it for a year based on the standard real-life-test period. At other times, passports have been issued for a full ten year term in the new name and gender based on simply a judge's Final Decree, as described above, and perhaps a letter of explanation. In the worst case, a new passport will always be issued in the new sex after sex reassignment surgery.

Insurance

Changing your name and gender identity on car, health and life insurance normally requires a Judge's Order. With some extra correspondence, the insurer can be made to accept a lawyer's Common Usage letter as well. While insurers will reflect a change of name and gender identity on your policy, they will probably be reluctant to re-rate you in the different sex. For a sex-based re-rating, insurers will require a letter from a doctor that you are biologically of the new sex. This can be accomplished after SRS. However, the insurer may required you to reapply in the new sex, and then refuse to insure you.

For car insurance, there is usually no difference in rates between sexes after 30-something. If you are at a sex-differentiated rate age, and a car insurer refused to re-rate you in the new sex, you could always apply to a different insurer in the new sex from the beginning. Make sure you have first changed your driver's license and your car title *before* you start making changes with the car insurance company.

For life insurance, a change in your sex should not affect your right to receive benefits. You are still the same person. Insurers, however, will be most reluctant to re-rate you in the new sex. If this is important to you, your best recourse may be to reapply for life insurance elsewhere in the new sex, perhaps after sex reassignment surgery. Women pay higher premiums for disability insurance; men pay higher premiums for life insurance.

For health insurance, a change in your sex will probably not be accepted for rate purposes unless it is certified by a doctor after sex reassignment surgery. Some correspondence and a Judge's Order will get the health insurance company to address you in your new name, and perhaps even put the proper "Ms" or "Mr." in front of it, but on their records you are likely to remain the sex you were at the time you applied for health coverage.

With insurance, you must always be aware of unintended results. Suppose you have a family health insurance policy. You dutifully notify your health plan that you have changed your name and sex, but remain happily married as a gay or lesbian couple. Their next response may well be that you can no longer be covered under a family policy because two people of the same sex can't be married. Whether or not the health insurer can get away with this depends upon your persistence, chance luck with the attitude of the health insurer's bureaucrats, and finally, if it goes this far, the decision of a judge.

If you already have health and life insurance, one legal strategy may be to change your name but not your sex with these firms. It may simply not be worth the risk to rock the boat. This will in no way undermine the legality of your name and sex change elsewhere. One can be a woman for the purposes of say health insurance, and a man for all other purposes. Always feel free to make maximum use of the ambiguity between the words gender and sex. If the insurer says "Well you must have changed your sex if your name was Jane and now is Jack." You could respond, at least while preoperative, "No, I've changed my gender, not my sex."

Wills, Trusts and Real Estate Ownership

Changing your name and sex on wills, trusts and real estate documents has no affect on your property rights whatsoever. If someone challenges whether or not Jack Frost has the right to property bequeathed to Jane Summer, he only needs to show his Judge's Order to proved that Jack Frost and Jane Summer are one and the same person. No change at all, just different sex. Similarly, a will made by Jane Summer and forgotten about is still fully enforced after death even though she died as Jack Frost.

On the other hand, if a will specifies a clear intent to only bequeath property to a person if they disavow a pre-existing transsexual tendency, then the decedent's intent will probably be respected. For example, if Grandpa Joe hated Jane Summer's transsexualism, and conditioned his bequest to Jane on her "never becoming a man in any way," Jack Frost would probably not be able to take possession of the inheritance. This would be especially true if he completed his sex reassignment surgery, since his maleness would be almost irrebuttable at that point.

An interesting situation arises regarding property held by a married couple in a community property state. If one of the couple transitions to the same sex as the other spouse, one could argue that all property acquired thereafter is not community property because people of the same sex cannot be married. This argument is not very strong because unless and until they get officially divorced, they are still legally married. Marriage, if valid initially, can only be ended by death, divorce or annulment. It is possible for two people of the same sex to *be* married; it is just not possible for two people of the same sex to *get* married.

Marital Rights or Divorce

During transition one needs to decide whether or not they want to stay married or get divorced. If divorce is the decision, then one needs to go through all the normal divorce procedures, as to which the transsexualism of one spouse should be irrelevant.

The only time that the transsexualism of one spouse arises as a divorce issue concerns the child custody. Whether or not a person's transsexualism affects their child custody rights depends on the attitude of the judge, and the quality of one's attorney. There are several legal cases in which transsexual parents received joint and even sole custody, with the judge determining the transsexualism to be irrelevant. (See, e.g., **Christian v. Randall** 516 p.2d 132 (1973) (Joint custody granted) There are other law cases in which it appeared that a parent's transsexualism was held against them, but usually there were aggravating factors in these cases, such as drug dependency. (**Daly v Daly**, 715 p.2d 56 (1986) (joint custody denied)

The legal standard for child custody is whatever is in the best interests of the child. If a transsexual is a good parent, and obtains a good attorney well-versed in transsexual issues to represent their interests, then there is an excellent chance that the transsexual will have at least joint custody.

If a couple decides to remain married, there are really no further legal issues at all. Transitioning and living as a same sex couple does not in any way invalidate a marriage. It takes a divorce, death or annulment to end a marriage. Marriages cannot be ended by changing gender identity or sex reassignment surgery. One cautionary note: married same sex couples should be careful in talking about their sex life. Sex between same sex (and different sex) couples can readily violate sodomy statutes still on the books in many states. An over-zealous sexist prosecutor might use sodomy as a basis for getting at a trans-sexual couple in his or her midst.

If a person transitioning is not married, but wants to marry during transition, there are several possibilities. First, the transsexual will only be able to marry someone if the two of them claim to be of different sex on their marriage license application. If the couple has the same kind of genitals before marriage, but claim to be of different sex, it is entirely possible that a judge will marry them without asking for ultimate proof such as birth certificate. In this case, it is clear that one of the partners would always have the right to annul the marriage, even if the transsexual later completes sex reassignment surgery, because it would be claimed that the marriage was not valid initially. While it could be claimed that the transsexual was of the sex claimed, but simply possessed a genital birth defect that was later corrected by SRS, nearly all judges would decide the sex claimed was not achieved until after the SRS. Hence marrying someone with the the same genitals during transition is somewhat risky, unless the couple lives happily ever after together.

It is also possible for someone in transition to marry someone with the opposite genitals. In this case the person in transition must claim to be the sex they are coming from. Such a marriage might also be annullable on one of two grounds. It could be claimed that the transsexual was really of their psychological sex, and hence the marriage was invalid as between two persons of the same sex, despite the difference in genitals. This argument would probably lose because, as noted above, judges will place great weight on the genitals in deciding which sex someone is. (See, e.g., **M.T. v. J.T.**,355 A.2d 204 (1976) (validity of trans-sexual marriage upheld.) A second ground for annulment would be that the non-transsexual spouse was defrauded into a same sex marriage. This argument would fail if it was clear that the non-transsexual spouse was well aware of the transsexual's nature.

To summarize, transitioning does not invalidate marriage. If the marriage doesn't work, divorce is always available. If a couple gets divorced, child custody is the only issue in which transsexualism gets involved. Transsexualism should not impede child custody if the transsexual is a good parent and gets a good lawyer to look after his or her rights. Getting married during a transition is also possible. However marrying someone with the same genitals will almost certainly result in an annullable marriage. This is true no matter how much a person believes they are of a different sex than that ordinarily indicated by one's genitals.

Which Washroom To Use When Not at Work or Home

Washroom laws usually don't exist. When they do exist, they apply only within the city limits of the jurisdiction that passed the law, and hence vary from town to town. As a result, it is impossible to provide general legal advice on which washroom to use when not at work. Also, practical considerations such as fear of embarrassment or concern for personal safety may far outweigh legal concerns. With these caveats in mind, we will nevertheless provide some guidelines for the transition period.

First if you are a transsexual in transition, and you need to use various washrooms, then be sure to carry with you at all times a psychologist's letter like the sample previously provided. This letter should prevent you from ever being convicted of a crime simply for using a washroom reserved for persons with different genitalia than yours. It shows that you had no intent to cause harm and were, in fact, simply following doctor's orders.

Second, use a washroom that is appropriate to your appearance. If you pass, then use the washroom that you pass for. If you don't pass, then don't use the washroom which is reserved for the sex you want to look like. You don't want to go through the hassle and embarrassment of being cornered by security, even if your psychologist's letter will get you off in the end.

Third, if you are not sure whether or not you pass, then use the washroom appropriate to the sex designation on your driver's license. Even if you get collared by security, it will probably be a brief matter if you can quickly show a driver's license that is appropriate to the washroom you want to use. Unless you get "busted" in the stall, it is very unlikely that someone would make you strip to prove your sex. All of this advice is premised on the understanding that one's behavior is bathroom appropriate at all times.

F - THE LAW AND THE TRANSSEXUAL DURING THE SURGICAL EXPERIENCE AND THE EARLY CONVALESENT PERIOD - M-F/F-M

The surgery is over. We are done with lawyers for good, right? Not necessarily. Unfortunately, there are instances of medical malfeasance in the field of transsexualism. If this happens to you, lawyers are the only people in the world that can help. Consider the following case involving Luis Suria, a 54 year old commercial artist and transsexual in New York City.

Suria, sometime in 1974, permitted silicone to be injected into each breast in the hope of forming female breasts. There was some dispute as to whether the silicone was injected by another transsexual friend, or by the defendant, Dr. Shiffman, in New York City. By March 1975, the breasts became inflamed, and Dr. Shiffman began injecting cortisone into the breasts to reduce the swelling. The cortisone had not helped much, and by July 1976 the silicone had solidified and hard nodules, called granulomata had formed, giving the breasts a hard, nodular, lumpy appearance. A few months later a surgeon and Dr. Shiffman performed an operation to drain the silicone. The patient claimed that the doctors said there would be just a small incision as a scar. Instead, there were extensive scarring and total disfigurement. Suria sued for medical malpractice and won a $1,500,000 award (later reduced to $800,000.)

The doctors claimed that Suria was responsible for her own injuries. They argued that she had caused the problem by injecting silicone into herself, and that they were simply trying to save her life by stopping the silicone from spreading to her other organs. But the jury was not impressed by this defense. Suria was awarded the damages because the jury did not believe that the doctors had given her an *adequate informed consent* -- that is, that they had not warned her that a consequence of the operation would be total disfigurement of the breasts. The fact that Suria may have caused her own problems was essentially irrelevant to the duty the doctors had to clearly inform her of the risks of what they were about to do with her body. As the judges in this case concluded:

"The duty to disclose risk is based upon a patient's right to determine what shall be done with his body. It is the physician's obligation to furnish a reasonable explanation of the available choices and potential dangers, the test of such reasonableness being for the jury to determine."

In essence, the jury in the Suria case believed that had Suria known what would happen to her breasts, she would not have undertaken the surgery with those doctors. As a result, the jury believed that Suria suffered $1,500,000 worth of harm.

The implications of the Suria case for the operative phase of transsexualism is to read the doctor's informed consent form carefully. If a risk is disclosed on that form, you will not be able to sue the doctor for it should that risk occur. If a tragedy occurs that was not disclosed by the doctor as a possible risk, then you will have a right to collect for the harm you have consequently suffered.

Informed Consent

An ethical surgeon will provide you with a long list of possible dangers and risks of transsexual surgery. Read the list carefully, realizing that any of those risks may happen to you. Based on what you read, you will be asked to sign an informed consent form. The form should not be very much different from the model informed consent form provided below. At minimum, the informed consent form should not require you to waive a right to sue for "negligence." When a surgeon conducts an operation in a way that a reasonable surgeon would not, and a patient suffers unintended harm thereby, then negligence may occur. It is alright to sign a waiver that says, in essence, "despite this surgeon's use of reasonable skill certain mishaps may still happen." It is not alright to sign a waiver that says, in essence, "this surgeon can be unreasonably sloppy with me and I still won't sue him or her." Do not waive your right to sue for negligence.

SAMPLE INFORMED CONSENT AND WAIVER OF LIABILITY

I, _____, having been fully informed in writing of the potential risks and complications of hormonal therapy or surgical sex reassignment, do hereby choose of my own free will and consent to undertake this treatment because I want to alter my physical appearance to more closely reflect my gender identity.

I hereby release Dr. _____ of any and all liability for my decision to undertake a change of my sexual appearance and, for long-term use of hormones or for sex reassignment surgery, to affect on a permanent, irreversible basis my current sexual functioning. I promise not to sue Dr. _____ for any of the consequences of my hormonal sex reassignment or surgical sex reassignment unless those consequences are the result of negligence in the conduct of my hormone therapy or in carrying out of my surgery.

Dated at _____, this _____ day of _____.

Patient Signature:_____

Witness: _____

If you are married, your surgeon may ask your spouse to sign a spousal waiver of liability. An example of such a letter is as follows:

SAMPLE SPOUSAL WAIVER OF LIABILITY

I, _____ am presently married to _____ ("Patient"). I understand that Patient wishes to alter his or her physical appearance to more clearly reflect his or her gender identity, and has been trying to do so for at least _____ year(s). I have been actively involved in, and fully support, Patient's sex change process.

I have been fully informed of the nature of transsexualism and transgendered surgery. I fully understand that the surgery or hormonal therapy which Patient will undergo will transform Patient into the opposite sex. I fully understand that the surgery and the effects of long-term use of the hormones is not reversible, and that patient will never be able to sire or bear children after the surgery or long-term hormonal therapy. I also understand that the sex reassignment process involves danger and risks, including, but not limited to, postoperative infection, depression, emotional changes and other physical and psychological changes. It is with my full knowledge and consent that my spouse, the Patient, undergo transgender surgery or hormonal therapy to cause a change of his/her sex to occur.

I hereby release and hold harmless Dr. _____ from any and all claims arising out of performance of transgender surgery or hormonal therapy, actual negligence excepted. I fully understand that I will not be able to seek monetary damages for any loss of sexual companionship between patient and myself, the loss of Patient's ability to sire or bear children or any similar problems which may arise from the performance of the transgender surgery or hormonal therapy.

Dated at _____, this _____ day of _____
Spouse Signature:_____
Witness:_____
NOTARY:

Postoperative Legal Notifications

There is no legal obligation to notify everybody that you have just had sex reassignment surgery. The mere act of sex reassignment surgery does not make one legally a member of a different sex. Your sex is ultimately a legal determination, and for a great many purposes that legal determination is made based on a birth certificate. Hence, one of the first things to do postoperatively is to get your surgeon to write a letter that he or she has successfully performed sex reassignment surgery upon you, transforming your sex to that of a male or female. Then take that surgeon's letter to the vital records office of the state in which you were born asking for a new birth certificate in your new sex.

If you had difficulty earlier getting a judge to change your gender identity in a Final Decree, getting a motor vehicle agency to designate "M" or "F" as you request, the surgeon's postoperative letter will solve those problems. Similarly, after SRS, the Passport Office will not hesitate to provide you with a normal duration passport in the new sex, although there is no legal precedent on this point.

The only real documentation difficulty you will encounter after SRS arises from the fact that some states provide you with a new birth certificate, some with only an amended birth certificate based on sex reassignment surgery. If you were born in one of the "new certificates" states, you completely lucked out. Those states are Illinois, New Jersey, Alabama, Hawaii, Maryland, North Carolina, Pennsylvania, Virginia. In those states, based on a surgeon's letter testifying to your SRS, a new birth certificate will be issued that looks like an original and shows your new sex.

If you were born in one of the "amended birth certificate" states (all others but Tennessee and Ohio,) you only have a problem if you mind having someone who must see your birth certificate knowing that you used to be a different sex. An amended birth certificate means that the registrar clearly indicates that the sex has been changed from what it was at birth. Generally this is no problem because it will only be shown to a judge or a bureaucrat. But it could be very embarrassing if one wants to hide their sexual past and the new birth certificate is seen by a new spouse or children.

If you were born in Tennessee or Ohio, too bad. Those are the only two states that will not issue even an amended birth certificate based on sex reassignment surgery. This can be a real problem if you need to show a birth certificate to get married, for example, and the marriage clerk sees that you and your fiancee have same sex birth certificates. Of course you could always get a judge's order in a different state, based on your SRS, stating you and your fiancee are differently sexed.

Another solution exists for persons born in Ohio or Tennessee, but it takes a bit of forethought. If you move to Holland for at least a year, and persuade doctors there that you are a transsexual, the you will qualify under Dutch law to have sex reassignment surgery in Holland. Dutch law further provides that transsexuals who receive sex reassignment surgery in Holland can receive an amended Dutch birth certificate in the new sex.

G - THE LAW AND THE TRANSSEXUAL DURING THE LATE CONVALESCENCE AND LIFE THEREAFTER - M-F/F-M

You are now healed from your surgery, and ready to take your rightful place in the world. Presumably all of your documentation is now in place. Most of it was taken care of during transition, and the SRS surgeon's letter hopefully pried loose a new or amended birth certificate. You've used that last piece of paper to clean up any documentary "holes" so that your sex is consistently "you" on all your records. In fact, it may be difficult from a paper trail to ever really discover what your previous sex was. Are you obligated to reveal this information? If so, to whom? What are the consequences for breach of privacy? These are the questions that this chapter addresses.

Generally speaking you may be under a legal obligation to reveal your sex reassignment surgery to someone if this information is reasonably necessary for a decision you are asking them to make on your behalf. There is no simple way to determine what is or isn't "reasonably necessary." Ultimately, in the case of a dispute, that question will be answered by a jury. However, you might ask yourself that if I was in the other person's shoes, is it reasonably necessary for me to know that a person asking me to do A, B or C had sex reassignment surgery? If the answer for you is yes, then you should reveal your information.

There are very few instances in which it is necessary to reveal sex reassignment surgery information. Once such instance, however, involves airline pilots. The reasoning here is that psychological stability and physical health is of paramount importance for an airline pilot. Hence an airline has a right to know a pilot's entire health history. One pilot that revealed her sex reassignment surgery and suffered the consequences was Karen Francis Ulane.

Before she changed her name and sex, Karen Ulane flew for Eastern Airlines. Her record as a male pilot was unblemished, and was preceded by a decorated career as an Air Force pilot. Ulane took a leave of absence in 1980 to have her sex reassignment surgery. When she recovered she passed a rigorous set of FAA psychological and physical health tests.

In 1981 she reported for duty at Eastern Airlines as a woman, and was promptly fired. The termination was eventually upheld on appeal, and Ulane soon died while testing an ancient DC-3 at a local airport. Ulane's termination was solely based on the perceived negative effect her transsexualism might have on other crew members and passengers. Ulane's lawyer claimed this was illegal sex discrimination. The Court of Appeals disagreed. They said that Eastern Airlines was discriminating based on *changing* of sex, not on sex *per se*. The court said that Congress never prohibited discrimination against changing of sex.

There was no way Ulane could have hid her sex reassignment surgery. But suppose she had her surgery at an earlier age, and failed to disclose it to a prospective airline employer. Would this be legal? Would it be ethical? Unfortunately, there are no clear answers to these questions. But consider the following. Today there are over two dozen known commercial airline pilots who are transsexuals. Airlines today such as American and Continental are more enlightened than Eastern was ten years ago. These successful transsexual pilots are Karen Ulane's legacy. But if any of them were to hide their transsexualism during the recruitment and application process, and it was later to be found out, they would certainly be fired for misrepresenting important health information on their employment application.

It might be thought that one has no greater obligation to reveal a transsexual past than that to a fiancee. But the courts have not found this to be the case for transsexuals, or for analogous situations involving gay men or lesbians.

In the case of **M.T v. J.T.**, a New Jersey Superior Court judge refused in 1976 to void a marriage because the husband learned only after the marriage that his spouse was a male-to-female transsexual. The Court reasoned that so long as the marriage was consummated -- as to which there was no dispute -- it was valid, and that whether the wife's vagina was there from birth or from surgery was irrelevant.

A different perspective is available in the case of **Baker v. Baker** from Brazoria County, Texas. This 1992 case involved an attempt by a wife to void a marriage to a female-to-male transsexual after they lived together for twelve years. The judge said that if fraud were involved an annulment would be possible, but only if it were raised shortly after the transsexualism was discovered. The judge implied that undisclosed transsexualism could be a kind of fraud, but in this case it was irrelevant because the spouse was aware of the situation for so long.

There a number of law cases involving attempts by one spouse to void a marriage when it is learned that the other spouse was or still is gay or lesbian. Judges reject all of these claims whenever there is evidence that the gay or lesbian spouse also consummated the straight marriage. This is similar to the finding above in J.T. v. M.T.

In summary, after sex reassignment surgery there is probably no legal obligation to reveal your past sex life to anyone. However, the failure to reveal your past to someone who has a legitimate interest in knowing it may entail certain consequences. One of those consequences is that you may be fired from a job, or dropped from an insurance policy. This would occur if you failed to reveal your SRS to employers or insurers that had a reasonable right to know. Another consequence is that your marriage may be voidable, and hence you could lose out on spousal support. But this consequence is less likely if your consummated the marriage as would any other member of your sex. Had you told your spouse of your sexual past, he or she would have no legal basis at all for subsequently claiming they were defrauded into marriage.

So long as your sex reassignment surgery is confidential, it is illegal under the confidential medical records provision of the Americans with Disabilities Act for others to reveal that information to anyone else. Sharing your sex reassignment surgery confidentially with an employer, insurer or spouse does not reduce the confidentiality of the information. In addition to civil and criminal penalties under the Americans with Disabilities Act, a transsexual would also be able to sue someone who wrongfully disclosed his or her medical record for tortious intentional infliction of emotional distress.

Other than concern for revealing or keeping confidential one's sex reassignment surgery, no other legal issues should arise long after convalescence. As with the real life test, most of the hard legal work is done before SRS -- documents, documents, documents. The surgery itself is momentous, and legally speaking it is most important to know what you got yourself into -- namely, to have given informed consent, without waiving suits for negligence. As the surgery fades into the past, so does the need for continued legal polishing of the gender transition. Your new persona is now complete, and the law is there to serve you in your new sexual identity, regardless of how it was achieved.

PART 3

Workplace Issues

SHEILA KIRK, M.D.
MARTINE ALIANA ROTHBLATT, J.D.

*"It's as if a large magnifying lens is being used
to look at you. An intense scrutiny takes place -
it all happens in the workplace -
more so than at any other time."*

H -THE TRANSITION PERIOD M-F/F-M

Preliminary Remarks

Employment! You need to plan, and plan, and plan again, before entering the transitional period. You and your mental health-care professional must address this time period very carefully and completely. Every detail about your training, capabilities, financial responsibilities, and closeup needs must be examined together. You should consider the very real possibility that you could lose your position, or that with transition, you could be transferred to a different location, or changed to a different kind of work. Quite possibly, you could earn a great deal differently than you did before you entered transition.

Your employer does not owe you this job and has by and large no legal or moral obligation to retain you. They may even sacrifice you no matter what your value and importance to the company, if they perceive that you could be a problem to the business, its customers or its workers. Your employer is in business and your change in role could be a real concern. Your employer will need vigorous reassurance that things in that business will not change. In fact, management will want reason to believe that things may actually improve, if that's at all possible. You will be hard put to prove and reprove your value to your company. Their tolerance level may be quite limited.

Hopefully as you enter transition, you will have all your appropriate documents changed. Certain basic changes are a must, i.e., social security name changed, appropriate changes to retain your pension and profit sharing status, bank accounts, etc. The mechanisms for this are provided elsewhere in this text. It is important that you attend to all this as you enter this time frame, if not just before.

For the M-F individual, it may seem not terribly important, but your facial electrolysis should be quite well along. Make up to cover a beard just won't do, and it won't last through a long work day. This vestige of the male is just as telltale and prominent as are the breasts of a genetic woman. You can't expect makeup to last and facial hair to stop growing for eight to ten hours every day.

When you enter the workplace in your new role, especially when you transition on the job, be prepared for the fact that acceptance of your coworkers will be at different levels and will take variable lengths of time from one to another. They may also be ambivalent. One worker may be moderately comfortable with you today and more than moderately uncomfortable with you tomorrow. Your patience and understanding will be strained at times. Don't lose control and to help in the rough times, be certain of the support system you have behind you outside of your work. Your family and friends are all important to you, at this time above all. If you are one of the fortunate people to have such a strong system, then you will weather the workplace storms much better. It is important also to realize that transition for some may last several years. We understand your impatience, but a slower transition may allow for a stronger integration. Rushing your transition at work may put more strain and reluctance on your coworkers. Keep this very much in mind.

To look at this in more depth, your pre-transition evaluation and therapy with your mental health-care professional should constantly consider your readiness, or lack of it for the transition entrance. There should be no premature moves to begin this time until absolute assurance on both of your parts is the case. Stop and think. Your ambivalence, your possible discouragement, reluctance and retreat back to your former gender role can be devastating to you and undermine considerably coworker acceptance and heighten their confusion. Be certain with your counselor as to where you are and when you are ready.

When you transition on the job, it's wise to consider the possible need of a conference between your mental health-care professional and your employer just after you have given that employer insight into your plan for a gender change. Your employer may find it helpful to you, and to your coworkers, to send them a written notice and explanation about you. And better to consider, is the scheduling of a meeting with those workers to discuss your altered role and your introduction to them. This preparation can make it much smoother for you. Your employer and counselor can make this introductory time far easier if they choose to help you in this way, and you should explore this avenue.

Also with a gender role change on the job, as the transition time progresses, periodic conferences with your manager, or supervisor, will be important not only to review your performance but also to evaluate your integration and pinpoint problems that you may not have insight into. It is also a very appropriate thing to keep your employer up to date about your plans for surgery, and while this is a very personal thing, and detailed discussion and information are not necessary, some insight into your plans are reasonable to share.

One last consideration before we move to consider specific issues for the M-F and F-M individuals -- Job descriptions are often very important to you and to your employer. Unions in the workplace demand them, workers are protected by them. But keep in mind that when you transition into the contragender role, your concept of that description may change from what it was before you entered this phase, and your employer's concept may not change. You both must have a meeting of the minds. In some forms of employment, i.e., factory work, or shipping departments, this can be a very important consideration, and if a union membership is involved, it could become really quite difficult.

CONSIDERATIONS FOR THE MALE TO FEMALE - M-F

When a person begins to live in the contragender role, when all their interactions with society and with family are in that contragender role, they are in the transition period. Some M-F individuals may choose to transition in the very same position, job, or company where they have been employed before they undertook this process. Others for many reasons may begin, and/or continue transition in a brand new position or even a brand new line of work. Each carries with it, several different considerations, and we should examine these different situations completely.

Experiencing transition on the job

In a sense, transitioning on the job, or same company, can be a more difficult proposition for the M-F individual. She is leaving, in fact, abandoning the men in the office or department to join the "other side." And the "other side" may have great difficulty in accepting her as well. To leave the men behind means probable loss of friendships, and even a perceived diminution in ability and integrity. The women will consider the new-comer still a male, especially if male attitudes are not changed, and they will more often than not resent the "masquerade" of this male in women's clothes. In short, the M-F individual challenges, and at the same time will be the recipient of challenges coming from both sides. In the estimate of some men, that individual has "stepped down." In the estimate of some women, that same individual can't learn what **they** know, think and experience because that person wasn't **born** a woman.

Transitioning on the job is hard also because you must satisfy your employer even more than before. You may have a key position, or be a very specially trained individual in your company and past performance has proved your capabilities and skill. In a word, you are vital to the organization and to lose you could lose market position or efficiency for your company. They will want to be satisfied that you are the same person, that you are still loyal, and that you will work for them as energetically as before. They want assurance that you are not going to disrupt operations in your unit or department, that you will not distract or alienate your coworkers. They want things to be as before -- but let's face it -- they aren't going to be as before. In every sense, each person in your company or office will have an issue with you. For some, the solutions will be simple. For some, solutions will be difficult and even near to impossible. What to do!

An option that may not present itself often is possible with a large company. You could be transferred to another division, or even another city, to continue in the same company. Your work history would go with you. Your new identity would be known to a choice few in that new position, and your path could be a bit simpler. Whatever takes place, the burden on you will be extraordinary, and you must plan for it. You must be willing to work with it in the most well thought out ways and be resourceful to meet all situations with comfort and dignity, as well as with tact.

When you first discuss with your employer your plans to transition, expect a number of discussions to follow. Punctuate them with literature that gives factual and supportive information about the transgendered person. It could be a great help to future discussion. Expect surprise, expect reluctance to accept, even rigidity and worse, even recrimination. But your manner, your ability to explain and inform and your reminder of your loyalty and efforts of the past will go a long way to put things into a better light. You may need to sit with several people in different levels of management very soon after the first conference. Your planning for more discussions and your experience with them will depend on the size and configuration of your company and your estimate of the personalities of the people you will hold discussion with. Remember, you are teaching, hence, use diplomacy and tact, but remember also that you are a person of dignity and worth. You are not coming "from behind" and once more, your value to them in your work and in your potential must be a part of the discussion.

In these meetings you will need to reassure that your change in clothing, your change in appearance and manner, will not disrupt and distract your coworkers. That is not altogether true, however, for a time, there may be some change in their attention to their work and their ability to relate to you comfortably. Nonetheless, you must reassure your employer that it will be business as usual, and they will look also to be reassured rather continuously for some time to come. Some of those superiors may be harder to convince, and slower to accept. If your boss is male you may threaten his masculinity in those sessions just as notably as you may threaten the other men in the workplace who will be in more contact with you and for longer periods of time. If your superior is a woman, your task may be a bit more difficult - she may reject you even more.

One very big hurdle then to overcome is to give information and reassurance to your employer and then make every effort to do your job and to do it well. This will take effort and stability, as well as confidence, perhaps more than you ever had before the transitional period.

One must think of the customers that you will have to interact with should your position put you into a public contact, either in person or by phone. How will you deal with this? What will your employer think about this particular circumstance, and when it comes to the bottom line, what kind of planning will you both embark upon in order to carry on business appropriately? This may take a good deal more discussion and planning, and it could prompt a change in your routine work even though you will be retained in the very same company. These are problems that can be solved. With accepting and responsible employers, any problem is solvable. Once again, reassurance of management of your loyalty, your continuing efficiency and dedication, will lead to finding solutions.

Your approach to your male coworkers and their approach to you is the next very large obstruction. There will be a number of reactions to respond to -- shock and disbelief, resistance to accept, out and out rejection and hostility, remarkable resilience and acceptance, and at times tolerance mixed generously with wariness. You have walked away from them. Old friendships can be shattered, never to be repaired. Stronger bonds can develop. A host of emotional and intellectual scenarios will result when they get the news. Some may have suspected or even known, but all will respond in some way.

You may need to give explanation and education. Your skill to give facts, accuracy and insight may be put to the limit. To know the transgendered community and explain it may be vital. To know yourself and how you fit into that population is also of extreme importance. A lot of this should be prepared for in your evaluation and study with your therapist. Bringing meaning, wisdom, and accuracy to your discussion of self and the transgendered is mandatory, and you can be a great help to your position and to the understanding of the transgendered community in what you say and how you say it. Remember, your words may be carried into discussion. Your coworkers may speak among themselves when you are out of earshot. They'll take those discussions to restaurants and bars and living rooms, barber shops, clubs and golf courses. Each man may discuss this with his wife, or girlfriend, or racquetball buddy. He may even discuss it with his bartender and all of them may have opinions. The accurate information you give to that coworker, hopefully may be shared with others as well. What you say may go all over their individual worlds.

Be the friendly, cooperative and generous person you were before you gave them this news, but keep in mind, some of your days will be miserable and trying, with one or several confrontative male coworkers. You must have the confidence and patience, stability and tact to handle it. You must know that short of an all out confrontation, you have to have the courage to come back the next day to perhaps face it all again. Men may be puzzled - why did you do this? It must mean that you are homosexual. They may wonder if you will "come on to them" and make them embarrassed in front of their coworkers. If they are friendly with you, they may very well be the butt of jokes from their coworkers. They may ask themselves -- how can they work with you at the same level as they did before. They can't take you into their confidence, or share a joke, or a piece of gossip with you any longer. They won't want to discuss last night's basketball game with you anymore. You don't fit in any of their involvements or interests. You have joined the "other side."

Look at how much healing you must do, and you must do it for if you don't, you will suffer, your coworkers will suffer, and the work of the company very probably may suffer. With that sequence of events, you can be discharged. No one can enumerate all the contingencies and situations you may encounter as you work with your male coworkers. You must devise, improvise, create, and rebuild, and still do the job you were hired to do. Keep in mind these thoughts, however.

1. You are not a siren, and you are not a glamour queen, nor are you a sex goddess. Your appearance and attitude must never give these impressions. Your comportment, your verbal exchange and your clothing must be as that of every other woman in that establishment. Good taste in keeping with the attitudes and habits of the other women there will earn you many points from both sides.

2. You must never come on to any male coworker. In reality, you should never date anyone in your department, or even in your company.

3. Always function with tact and with confidence. Keep a handle on your temper and your attitude. Give information when necessary, but don't be a missionary. You do not have to give every detail, or speak at great length about your feelings or your plans. Always show willingness to work efficiently and with capability. This will profit you well when working with the males in your workplace, and certainly will be important for your superiors to observe. Will all of this work out well for you in the end? Very probably it could, but it won't be easy.

The very biggest of hurdles for you to face and overcome will be your interaction with the women in your unit or office. Some few will have remarkable compassion and acceptance. They will prove to be your supports and friends. Don't overindulge in their openness, however do accept it all with friendliness and warmth. Again, don't take advantage. They will be a great help to you in your work and as time goes on, they will be your aids to moving further into that special circle.

Those who resist will do so with a number of motives. Associated with all those motives is the fact that you were not born to this place in life, no matter how strong your gender identity. No amount of hormonalization or surgery is going to change that fact. Even if you master every nuance of fashion, hair care, make up and body language, there is one factor that will keep you out of that special society of women. It is the fact that you came from a different culture, that of the male. Even more, you may never know in your interaction with women whether you are accepted because you are a woman, or because you are a very successful and polished transsexual. That is a rather difficult burden to carry, but this is one of the problems with transitioning on the job and you must face that.

Certain and very important concepts
and principles to keep firmly in mind always:

A. Your mode of dress, hair care and make up, your appearance, your visual credibility -- all of this is most important. You must never be provocative and never, never dress in a sexy way. The most attractive woman selects her clothing with good taste and care. Her clothing fits properly and is never overly revealing. She dictates a fashion as is appropriate to her age, and a good rule to keep in mind is that a 55 year old does not dress like an 18 year old. Your make up and hair style should fit with the kind of work or position you occupy in the workplace. Theater techniques are never to be used. You will be judged severely by your female coworkers, if you don't keep these things in mind. You will distract them and the men in your department. They will joke about you and your superior may call you in and spell it out for you. This appearance will be looked on as flamboyant and an interference with the work of the business. It won't be tolerated. The very group you want most to accept you, to embrace you, and to help make it all very easy, will turn their backs on you.

B. Your speech, attitude and body language must be as authentic as possible. You may anticipate having voice therapy, or even voice modulation surgery, but likely you won't be quite that far along when you begin transition. If you speak as a man does, with low voice pitch, with very characteristic masculine phrasing and inflection, you can try and change some of this early in the transition. Visits with a vocal therapist or speech pathologist will help greatly. How much success you will have is variable, but keep this in mind. Soft spoken individuals command more attention than those with loud, heavy voices. Spontaneous and feminine gestures along with body position and movement also go a long way to authenticate the person. You may have absolute taste in your wardrobe, but if in your sitting positions, your walk, your hand movements, and the like, you indicate that you are a typical male, the image is shattered. Your comportment is very important. Learning and blending it into your everyday function is vital. These small and sometimes hardly discernable nuances detract from the voice and fortify the image of femaleness. You will need to sharpen your sense of observation in watching women. Observe them everywhere, in restaurants, on buses, on the street, and particularly -- in the workplace.

C. Develop your sense of the female culture, that special society. This more than anything else that we have looked at to this point is the most critical ingredient in your approach to acceptance. Women have a special bond, uniting each and every one, and no matter what society, culture, country or business position they come from, they understand it and are a part of it. It's a bright ribbon and they all grasp it quite firmly. They know with great empathy the pleasures and comfort of good gynecologic health and they discuss it. They know also the rigors of poor obstetrical experience and they reach out to each other whenever they observe it in another or experience it in themselves. They instinctively know how to connect and negotiate, how to interact and how to share. Women come from a very different place and are of a very different "stuff" than are men.

When I refer to all of these things, I speak of a special society that women belong to. Just being a genetic woman gives her credentials to be a member. You have to learn it all. You have to understand and then apply the many rules and travel the mental, emotional, and spiritual pathways that women travel. If you don't have a mind to look into discovering as much as is possible in that culture, you are forever lost and forever locked out.

It is very important that you begin to know the medical problems of women, especially as they relate to obstetrical and gynecological issues in their lives. If you are not to be known as a new woman, you may need to fashion a believable story about your experience with menstruation and possibly sexually transmitted disorders. It will be important that you have some insight into women's response and experience with sexual matters, and be ready to discuss them. Other aspects of women's health are vastly important to have information about. For instance, breast diseases and mammography experiences, hysterectomy and urinary tract infections, as well as vaginal monilial infections and anemia. All of these are areas of very common concern and experience in all women. These areas of information may not be pertinent when you are known to be in transition, but when you are in work or in social situations where your original role is not known, you must be knowledgeable, and you may need to have a logical and believable history of your own health history. Women share their obstetrical experiences, and they speak to each other constantly about children, the problems with their growth, and their own individual techniques in rearing and nurturing. You will need to prepare for this, and as we have indicated before, so much more has to do with personal female health and the health of others in the female's life.

Several additional points to keep in mind:

1. Women often find something complimentary about one another. They look at the other's hair style and lip color. They observe their dress, shoes and jewelry. In most instances, they give a compliment. You should do it as well. To tell a female coworker how nice she looks today or that you admire her earrings can be a beautiful start to a good relationship, not only that day, but for the future. Don't over do it - you don't want to create the impression of a "come on."

2. Put a clamp on expressions, male mannerisms and discussion techniques. Don't overpower or dominate in conversation. Don't superimpose your opinions or experiences. You win no friends and you influence no one when

you do these things. Don't believe either that your experiences and success in business as a male will carry you fully in this transition as a women. Both the men and the women will not allow it. The men see you as one who has abandoned your masculinity. They may even believe that you have lost your business skills. The women will not tolerate your masculine attitude and techniques in your new role. In short, the old attitude and the new role do not mix at any time and in any way. Experience will be appreciated when offered correctly. "Attitude" will never be acceptable.

3. Build friendships with other women and try to connect with acquaintances, but don't overdo it and don't retreat into a solitary place. Women share and interact, men characteristically do not share and interact. Often when interaction is necessary, they do it with reluctance and hesitancy, if at all. The skills women utilize must be learned and adopted by you.

4. When asked for information and explanation of what it is that you are doing and experiencing, be prepared to be factual and give all that is required. Once again, don't become a missionary. Don't over instruct and don't preach.

When transitioning on the job, an advantage can be gained when you have one or several real friends in both the male and female groups in the workplace. They can be guides in many ways for you. They can give you encouragement and critique. They can help you with your need to adjust in many different ways and they often times can offer insight into your successes and failures. As in all times in our lives, true friends however are not always that common.

Experiencing transition in a brand new workplace

When you transition in a different area of work or in a brand new workplace where you are not known, one of the very real problems that you will face is that you may have no real work history to use in order to promote yourself. This becomes a problem right from the very start, for it may lead to an open declaration of who and what you are at the initial interview with your employer or very soon thereafter. If you are looking to enter that particular work force without giving yourself away, you are stopped cold by this. Personal references are not difficult to supply. Hence, testimony of your loyalty, honesty, steadfastness and reliability can be supplied quite easily. Your problem however may be in offering substantial evidence of your performance in the workplace. In most instances, that performance was in the gender that you have left behind.

You face a difficult decision. If you plan to hide your past and your chances of doing so are better than good, because you pass in appearance and in cultural adaptation, then you run risks. The greatest disaster will be that if you are exposed at some time in the future, you likely will be discharged on the spot because you have deceived your employer. It won't matter how exceptional you are in your work, you will be gone! Some in transition are willing to take that chance. Only you can be the one to decide just what the risks of this approach really are. You are on your own in this decision.

As hard as it will be, you probably should consider giving honest insight into who you are, provided that insight stays with your interviewer or is shared with only one or two very necessary people. That honesty will be to your great credit. An inquiry can be made of past employment giving a continuity and appraisal of your abilities and talents to your potential employer.

Now that's challenging, isn't it? - but there will be no surprises ahead for you or the employer. Then you can set to work when hired to show your great abilities. As always, by being an excellent team worker, by being compatible and by fitting into both the male and female groups, you can go very far in the job.

What if by some chance you are exposed by a coworker, or a leak from the top. Once again, all the points you have assembled because of your good work and comfortable personality may go right out the window. Coworkers who are shallow, rigid in their views and steeped in prejudice will make your life difficult. Once again, your tact, willingness to discuss and confidence in yourself will be called upon to the maximum, and you will be thrown into the same position you would be in if you transitioned on the job. It won't be easy. Your patience, endurance and your attitude will be critical factors in your survival.

The bathroom question - your problem or theirs!!

In reality, it is a problem for all concerned. Agreeable solutions are often hard to come by. If at all possible, a single commode facility someplace on the premises would be a solution. This won't always be available to you. If you are in transition and preoperative, you are unacceptable in both restrooms. If you are postoperative, there is no question and no discussion. You must use the women's rest facilities. So then this is an issue for you while you are in transition. How do you satisfy yourself and your coworkers in this problem? You and your employer will need to evaluate thoroughly the options and a policy will be established that is not to be questioned, or altered, no matter what your coworkers may feel or how they object. Your coworkers must accept employer decision. That decision means use of the female facilities in some specific location and perhaps in a special time plan. It must be clearly understood by your coworkers that those facilities are to be used by you **and** by them for the exact same reasons, nothing more, nothing less. Will that plan adopted by your employer suit everyone? Probably not. There is always going to be an objector. You may need to seek out that person(s) and discuss tactfully what they find a problem. More often than not, their objections are so strong because of other deep seated concerns. Discussion with them could help to diffuse the whole situation. Again your tact and ability to teach and persuade is all important.

Locker rooms may carry somewhat more concern on the part of your female coworkers. Again, an appropriate plan worked out by you and your superior will be needed and then explanation to your coworkers will be a must. The plan you adopt will always be unique to your particular workplace. Time schedules may be the solution. Other solutions of course are possible. In time, your acceptance as you perform your duties and "mix" with your coworkers, the bathroom and locker room questions will become less and less an issue and the problem will go away.

CONSIDERATIONS FOR THE FEMALE TO MALE IN THE TRANSITION PERIOD - F-M

Experiencing Transition on the Job

The transition period for you may not be quite as challenging a time as it is for the M-F person. Genetic women can dress androgenously and wear their hair in styles approaching the masculine with less challenge than the M-F person. But there is no doubt you will want to enter the transition period with as complete a persona and spirit of the male as is possible and it is to your advantage to do this relatively soon so as to eliminate confusion and not to delay the acceptance process. While you can afford to move more slowly and with more deliberation in the transition period than your M-F counterpart (and it often times does benefit you to do so since slow integration is much easier on those around you,) still the transition period is a time to adapt, adjust and to integrate. Half measures and half efforts can't be allowed for too long.

Some F-M individuals may choose to transition on the job. Others will choose a new company or even a new line of work. Each carries with it several different considerations, and we must examine these different situations quite completely.

In a way, the on the job transition could be somewhat more difficult for the F-M person. He is leaving the society of women and their culture and moving to the "other side." The men on the other side may have great difficulty in accepting him because they fear that this person is still a woman and not privileged to enter into their conversation and plans. The F-M is betraying one group of coworkers and seems to have no right to join the other. Language and ways of expression are different, and the sexual overtones that are often a part of a man's exchange with a male coworker, either overt or covert, can not be used with this new "member" of the male sex. A male just can't comfortably talk with a F-M person about wanting a sexual interlude with some female in the workplace. He can much more easily with another genetic male. In brief, the challenges from both sides offered to you are far greater than the challenges that perhaps sometimes you offer to them. It is true, you have "stepped up" on the ladder and that is considered good, but good only with qualification.

Another major problem when transitioning on the job is the need to satisfy and reassure your employer. You may have a key position or be a very specially trained individual in your company, and past performance has proved your capabilities and skill. In a word, you may be vital to the organization and to lose you could lose market position or efficiency for your company. But they will want to be satisfied that you are the same person, that you are still loyal, and that you can work for them as before. They want assurances that you are not going to disrupt operations in your unit or department. They want to know that you will not distract or alienate your coworkers. They want things to be as before - but let's face it, they aren't going to be as before.

An option that may not present itself often is possible with a large company. You could be transferred to another division, or even another city, to continue in the same company. Your work history would go along with you. Your new identity would be known to a choice few in that new position, and your path could be just a bit simpler. This is a possibility to consider when entering the transition period. The burden on you will be extraordinary, and you must plan for it. You must be willing to work with it all in the most well thought out ways and be resourceful to meet all situations with comfort, dignity, and with tact.

When you first discuss with your employer your plans to transition, expect a number of discussions to follow. Punctuate them with literature that gives factual and supportive information about the transgendered person. Expect surprise, expect reluctance to accept, even rigidity, and worse, even recrimination. Your manner, your ability to explain and inform, and your reminder of your loyalty and efforts of the past will go a long way to put things into a better light. You may need to sit with several people in different levels of management very soon after the first conference. Your planning for more discussions and your experience with them will depend on the size and configuration of your company and your estimate of the personalities of the people you will discuss with. Remember, you are teaching - use diplomacy and tact, and remember that you are a person of dignity and worth. You are not coming "from behind" and once more, your value to them in your work and in your potential must be a part of the discussion.

In these meetings, you will need to reassure that your change in clothing, your appearance and manner, will not disrupt and distract your coworkers, at least not for very long. You must reassure your superiors that it will be business as usual, and they will look to be reassured rather continuously for some time to come. Some of those superiors may be harder to convince, and slower to accept. The important things then to remember, are to give information and reassurance to your employer and to do your job and do it well. It will take more effort and stability, as well as confidence, and more of these than you ever had in the pre-transitional period.

And what of the customers that you may be in contact with should you be in a position which puts you into public contact, either in person or by phone. How do you deal with that? What will your employer's thinking about this when it comes to the bottom line of carrying on the business. This may take even more discussion and planning, and it may prompt a change in your routine work even though you will be retained in the company. These are problems that can be solved. With accepting and responsive employers, any problem is solvable. Once again, reassurance of management of your loyalty, your continued efficiency and dedication will lend all that is needed to find solutions.

The next very real hurdle will be your approach to your female coworkers and their approach to you. The women that you work with, some of whom that have become more then just acquaintances, may respond with shock and disbelief. They may be openly hostile. They may delay acceptance, or they perhaps may give it freely. Some women with their intuitive sense may have put clues together and your transition will not be a surprise to them. But most, if not all, will have resentment and regret to some degree. You are forsaking them and leaving their culture. They may even believe you are abandoning friendships and they will suspect you. Their ability to be all out nasty, mean, to gossip and backbite could make life very difficult. They may display degrees of confusion and discomfort and former closeness with many could disappear. Your learned skills for connecting and interaction can help greatly in the process. Use your own insight and intuition to advantage. Blend the female methods of negotiation with the male initiative to provide avenues for open exchange. You need to problem solve with the women you work with, to approach them with techniques they understand and utilize themselves. What a fabulous position you are in, for you know these methods (the M-F person must learn them and may never learn them well.)

You can reassure, convince, and teach with effectiveness and your levels of success can be judged by how well you break down the resistance and how effectively you rekindle the friendships that you had. If not handled sensitively all that you do however will place you in their estimate as someone who has run away from them, and you are now a male figure.

You will need to give explanation and education. Your skill to give facts, accuracy and insight will be put to the limit. To know the transgendered community and explain it will be vital. To know yourself and how you fit into that population is also of extreme importance. A lot of this should be prepared for in your psychologic evaluation and study with your therapist. Bringing meaning, wisdom, and accuracy to your discussion of self and the transgendered population is mandatory, and you can be a great help to your position and to the understanding of the transgendered community in what you say and how you say it. Remember, your words will be carried into discussion by these women, in the workplace when you are out of earshot. They will bring these discussions home to share with husbands and with boyfriends. They will discuss it in restaurants, at church and at club meetings. The people that they will share with, telling them about you, will often have no information or worse, misinformation and they will have opinions as well. What you give to your coworker must be accurate and positive.

Be the friendly, cooperative and generous person you were before you gave them this news, but keep in mind, some of your days will be miserable and trying, with one or several confrontative coworkers, and you must have the confidence and patience, the stability and tact to handle it. You must know that short of an all out confrontation, you must have the courage to come back the next day to perhaps face it all again. There will be a great deal of healing for you to do, and you have to do it, for if you don't, you will suffer. Your coworkers will suffer and the work of the company will suffer as well and you could be discharged. No one can forecast all the contingencies and situations you will encounter as you work with the female coworkers at your job. You must devise, improvise and create, and rebuild, and still do the job that you were hired to do. Keep in mind these thoughts, however:

1. Use your feminine abilities to help the women around you accept you as a male. It sounds ridiculous but it is true. You have techniques to bring them to acceptance. Their reluctance may be great, but you will have already in place the abilities to insure their comfort and change their attitudes.

2. There will be gradual but distinct changes in your physical appearance that they can and will accommodate to. They will see them. Once on a hormonal regimen with gradual development of facial hair and a deepening of your voice, you will confirm your plans and goals to all around you. This could be for some a cause for ambivalence and a few may return to a hostile and defensive position. This could resurrect old discussions and old problems may have to be managed all over again.

Your interaction with the male coworker will probably be the biggest problem that you will face when you transition on the job. You are seeking to enter a society of individuals who really suspect you and for a long period may reject you because you don't know their motivations, drives and mechanisms to relate to one another. That is what they think. That certainly is not really true, is it? You have been watching and interrelating with men for years before this transition period. You know quite well how they think and what they think. You could be quite a surprise to them.

Yet they may resist for they may still think of you as a female. You may have been a sex object for several and now you want to be one of them. That could challenge those individuals because you challenge their sexuality, and that hits them where they "live." They will wonder if they are homosexual. They may resist you more for this than anything else. Men as you know, are competitive and they may resent you for what you bring to this particular job. If it is more than they are capable of bringing to the job, you will be more out of the loop and out of the group. You will need to use skill to maintain your productiveness and inventiveness and yet to have every ability to build friendships within the men's groups. However, men's concept of friendship is nothing like the friendship built between women. That is an important fact you need to keep in mind and your outreach to build friendships in the same way can sometimes fall very hard to earth. Friendships are built in totally different ways between men. Most of the time it is not a sharing of past experiences that have been primarily emotional. Friendships between men are built on the basis of common goals, common competitive schemes and skills, and once common goals are accomplished, often times friendships either fade away or become far less intense.

You've observed but you will need to remember. Men must achieve, must accomplish, must be in the forefront and if not at the top, very near to it. If you act in the same way you may be challenged severely. If you attempt to do it using the same mechanisms, you will not always be assisted. That's a hard problem to resolve -- isn't it? Not all men act this way, it is true and if in your work group there are those that don't, you will be very gratified and life can be a lot easier. But most of them do thrive on competition and one upmanship.

Men will discuss and plan together but not as women do. Remember that a lot goes unsaid in men's verbal exchange. They assume, they fail to share, they don't want to go into great detail and above all, they don't want to exhibit emotions and feelings as women do. Generally, their range of emotions has to do with anger, defiance, hostility and even at times, physical exchange. There is no doubt that under the effects of your hormonal regimen, many of these approaches will be incorporated into your personality. You certainly must learn not to exhibit emotions and feelings as only women can. You must put a brake on that mechanism. However, don't discard it. Save it rather for that special relationship, or for the family/friendship circle supporting you.

Be prepared for the "test." It will always be there. Testing will go on and on even when you have proved yourself repeatedly. Someone will put you into that testing. They will want to be satisfied that you know what is needed for this performance or that. They will want to know that you can bring to the job the right conclusion and that you are up to new and innovative plans. They want to be certain that you will contribute as do all the other males in the office. The very biggest of tests will be how you exchange in conversation as males do. Will you tell jokes? Will you be able to pass comments about sexual matters in reference to this woman or that in workplace? *(After all, you were a woman once and it will be interesting for them to observe whether or not you consider women as men do.)*

The men around you in the workplace may challenge you far more than the women in that particular job setting. You seek to join their special culture and you will be asked to prove that you can belong, a great many times.

When transitioning on the job, there are notable problems, but an advantage can be gained when you have one or several real friends in both the male and female groups of that particular workplace. They can be guides in certain ways. They can give you encouragement and critique. They can help you in your need to adjust in different ways and can give you insight into your successes and failures. As in all times in our lives, true friends are not common.

Experiencing Transition In A Brand New Workplace

If you are quite well along in your masculinizing hormone regimen and even more if you have had breast removal surgery, your ability to "pass" is virtually guaranteed. You don't face the problems that the male to female individual faces in appearance. You are male in face and voice and you can feel extremely confident. What confronts you however is the following. When you transition in a brand new workplace where you are not known, or in a different area of work, one of the real problems that you will face is that you may have no real work history to use to promote yourself. This can lead to open declaration of who and what you are at the initial interview or very soon thereafter. If you are looking to enter that particular work force without giving yourself away, you are stopped cold by this. Personal references are not difficult to supply. Your problem may be in offering the substantial evidence needed of your performance in the workplace prior to coming to this position, and in most instances, that performance was in the gender that you have left behind.

You face a difficult decision. If you plan to hide your past and your chances are doing so are better with the passage of time and continuance of your hormonal regimen, and you can pass in cultural adaptation, then you run risks of a different nature. The greatest disaster will be that you are exposed at some time after you have begun in this new position and you could be discharged on the spot because you have deceived your employer. It won't matter how exceptional you are in your work, you will be gone! Some F-M individuals are willing to take that chance and only you can be the one to decide just what the risks of this approach really are.

As hard as it will be, you probably should consider giving honest insight into who you are, provided that insight remains with your interviewer or is shared only with one or two very necessary people. That honesty will be to your great credit. An inquiry can be made of past employment giving a continuity and appraisal of your abilities and talents to your potential employer.

That's very challenging, isn't it? But there will be no surprises ahead for you or for the employer. Then you can set to work when hired to show your great abilities and do so with ease. As always, by being an excellent team worker, by being compatible, and by fitting into both the male and female groups, you can go very far in the job.

What if by some chance you are exposed by a coworker, or a leak from the top. Once again, all the points you have assembled because of your good work and comfortable personality may go right out the window. Coworkers who are shallow, rigid in their views and steeped in prejudice will make your life difficult. Once again, your tact, willingness to discuss, and your confidence in yourself will be called upon to the maximum, and you will be thrown into the same difficulties you would be in if you transitioned on the job. It won't be easy. Your patience, endurance, and your attitude will be critical factors in your survival.

The bathroom question - your problem or theirs!!

In reality, it is a problem for all concerned. Although for the F-M individual, this does not loom as great a problem as it is for the M-F. Agreeable solutions are often hard to come by should there be objectors. If at all possible, a single commode facility someplace on premises would be a solution and could make things much more comfortable for you, and for others. This won't always be available to you. How can you satisfy yourself and your coworkers? You and your employer will need to evaluate thoroughly the options and a policy will be established that is not to be questioned, or altered, no matter what. Your co-workers must accept employer decision, and they must understand that your use of those facilities is for the exact same reason that they use them, nothing more, nothing less. When there does prove to be an objector, you may need to seek out that person and discuss tactfully what they find a problem. More often than not, their objections are as strong as they are because of other deep seated concerns. Discussion could help to diffuse the whole situation. Again your tact and ability to teach and persuade is all important.

Locker rooms may carry somewhat more concern for you than for your male coworkers. Again, an appropriate plan worked out by you and your superior will be needed and then explanation to those coworkers will be a must. Plans will always be unique to that particular workplace. Time schedules may be the answer. Other solutions certainly are possible. In time, your acceptance by your coworker will have a strong bearing on the bathroom and locker room issues, and the problem will go away.

Some concluding thoughts M-F/F-M

Transition is a frightful time and the challenges are formidable, but it is designed as it is to strengthen your resolve, to make you resourceful, to sharpen you and make you a survivor. When entering the workplace, you may find great changes in your work capacity or your acceptability. There may also be considerable changes in your level of income. These are cruel possibilities. Nonetheless, you and your counselor should have considered all of the possibilities and jointly have prepared for them.

It may be that schooling is needed to give you a new avenue to a productive and satisfying job. Earning a degree could be the answer. Learning a new skill could be a solution to the problems you face when trying to obtain meaningful employment. You may choose to put yourself in the job market as a temporary employee, or in a secretarial position, or as a part time employee in foods, or repair services. Some of these approaches could use your skills fully and be very remunerative and also offer a great deal less stress. Your early and very thorough investigation of your place in the labor force and all of the alternatives open to you is very important. Once there, your need is to adapt and to always give positive impression of your reliability, responsibility and loyalty.

I - After Surgery, In Early
Convalesence - M-F/F-M

When the time comes that surgery is planned, whether it be a major surgical procedure or a minor nature with short convalescence, you owe it to special people to tell them what you are doing. To give them great detail is not necessary, unless you feel that it is needed for one or several in particular. When your surgical schedule is decided upon, you need to determine how long you will be in the hospital, and how long you will be in convalescence at home. You need to have as accurate as possible information about return to work and what you will be allowed to do by your doctor. That information must be given to management. Obviously, minor procedures generally won't take you out of the work schedule for long, or keep you from the usual involvement there. Recovery from vaginoplasty or phalloplasty can be lengthy, and if complications take place, the recovery will be prolonged. The details of this must be given to your employer and can be given to a few friends of your choosing in the workplace as well.

You will need to determine what time is allowed you for sick and recovery time - whether or not vacation time will be used up, and if time for personal needs, when allowed to an employee of your firm, can be accumulated and added to sick time. The policy of your company should be well understood so as to make time allotment and to make your needs well understood. Sometimes a letter from your physician will be important to help clarify and make your request for time easily granted.

Most probably, long before your surgical plans are made, you will have looked into health care benefits as allowed to you by your company. You will know quite well where you stand on third party payment. Most of the time you are not covered. However, there are plans wherein surgery for reassignment is not covered, but then aftercare is because you are, in their criteria, now a new member of the other gender. It is worth inquiry about this. It is worth also updating your insurance allowances and coverage occasionally. Surprises could be in store for you.

During your home convalescence, it is worth sending a letter to your supervisor, or a key person in management, giving them insight into your level of recovery. Thank them for their support and their patience and be sure to indicate how close to your plan for return to work you are. If those plans are altered and the return date is delayed, tell them. Allow them time to plan and to make changes to keep their operation going smoothly. A phone call to one good friend in the workplace giving information about your recovery and your plans, will be very helpful to you. That friend can pave the way with coworkers to gain interest and support for you, and comfort with you on your return.

Once you are recovered adequately to return to work, it may be necessary to schedule only half days for the first week. Your doctor will advise you about this possibility and once again, a statement from him/her to your employer may be needed if that be the case. Be certain however, that you are ready to go back to the workplace. Be sure that you are ready and able to perform your duties completely and efficiently. It will be expected that you are prepared to do your job.

One last thought, if any postsurgical visits are scheduled during the work day, be certain to inform your employer of these visits well in advance. Don't overstep their generosity and try to schedule at off-work times. You are going to be drawn into conversations and explanations about what happened to you and what took place. Your judgement as to details is all important, but as before, be thoughtful of how much you say.

J - In Late convalescence and life thereafter - M-F/M-F

You have now settled down to living the rest of your life in a most appropriate way. You are now the person you know yourself to be. Possibly, there may be more medical and surgical care to face, but even if there is, you are very far along in your new gender role, whether on the same job or in a brand new type of work, a new career or a new company. You are in beautiful congruence with self. If there is more surgery to face, you can do it with confidence, more assurance, and so much more ability to plan with great determination to "reach for it all." You've moved into a wonderful place in your life, and all of life stretches out before you -- to enjoy, to experience to the fullest, and to explore. What a wonderful place you have come to!

For the New Woman - M-F

You may have decided to experience a bit more surgery and have decided to add a secondary cosmetic procedure to the genital reassignment. You may even plan to have some facial, or skull reconstructive surgery at a later date. You will need to save money for this. Likely it will still be an "out of pocket" payment, but you can do it. You saved once to do all before this. It can be done once again.

You can move into higher echelons of business. You can advance in the work-place in this job, or in another. You face some of the obstructions that society places in the path of women. Men in the workplace particularly, may impose great difficulties and restrictions. You can move past them however with your abilities, energy and intelligence. You can move ever upward. Women all around are overcoming. They are moving into management and better income in every phase of work, in every kind of company, in every occupation. You can add your efforts to that of your sisters in the workplace.

Your documentation is complete, your medical needs are worked out with a competent and empathetic physician. Now your social life begins in earnest. Your desire for more education may be important, and you should pay attention to this. Your relationships with family members and friends hopefully will be strengthened. You can pursue hobbies and sports as you choose. You can continue to blossom. You can move happily and comfortably. Your life has really developed into one of fulfillment, satisfaction and peace.

For the New Man - F-M

Your need for additional surgery and planned medical supervision may be some-what greater and somewhat prolonged than for the new woman. You will need to save for that additional care. But you can do that. You will be in a job or occupation that will permit you to do this, and you saved before, to come this far. You can do it again.

The workplace, the playing field, your family and your friends will be of great support and enjoyment to you. Give to them fully and expect that they will give just as much, and more in return.

Your performance in your work will help greatly to assure position, advancement and income. Don't lose sight of it. More education may be important. Don't hesitate to take advantage of it. You are in a superior position in the workplace. Society has ordained it to be so. Take advantage of it, but don't forget your ability to use what female qualities you were born with and all those methods that you developed prior to transition. That wonderful blend can work so positively for you.

Bring friends and family close to you if they will permit, and make them a part of this exciting phase of life. Stop and think, it is very exciting -- it's a time when fulfillment, satisfaction, and peace is yours.